THE HEART OF NATURE
Or The Quest For Natural Beauty

by

Sir Francis Younghusband

The Heart Of Nature
Or The Quest For Natural Beauty
by Sir Francis Younghusband

ISBN: 978-93-57487-83-2

Published by

DOUBLE 9 BOOKS

2/13-B, Ansari Road
Daryaganj, New Delhi – 110002
info@double9books.com
www.double9books.com
Tel. 011-40042856

ABOUT THE AUTHOR

Lieutenant Colonel Sir Francis Edward Younghusband was a British Army officer, explorer, and spiritual author. He was born on May 31, 1863, and died on July 31, 1942. People remember him for the trips he took to the Far East and Central Asia, especially the British expedition he led to Tibet in 1904, and for the books he wrote about Asia and foreign policy. Younghusband was a British commissioner to Tibet and the President of the Royal Geographical Society, among other jobs. Younghusband took a trip across Asia in 1886 and 1887 while he was still a young officer and on leave from his unit. Younghusband married Charles Magniac's daughter Helen Augusta Magniac in 1897. During the trip to Tibet, Vernon, who was Augusta's brother, worked as Younghusband's personal secretary. The couple lived in Westerham, Kent, from 1921 to 1937, but Helen did not go with her husband on his trips. Younghusband had a stroke in July 1942, right after he spoke at the World Congress of Faiths in Birmingham.

CONTENTS

INTRODUCTION

Town children let loose in a meadow dash with shouts of joy to pluck the nearest flowers. They ravenously pick handfuls and armfuls as if they could never have enough. They are exactly like animals in the desert rushing to water. They are satisfying a great thirst in their souls—the thirst for Beauty. Some of us remember, too, our first sight of snowy mountains in the Alps or in the Himalaya. We recall how our spirits *leaped* to meet the mountains, how we gasped in wonder and greedily feasted our eyes on the glorious spectacle. In such cases as these there is something in the natural object that appeals to something in us. Something in us rushes out to meet the something in the natural object. A responsive chord is struck. A relationship is established. We and the natural object come into harmony with one another. We have recognised in the flower, the mountain, the landscape, something that is the same as what is in ourselves. We fall in love with the natural object. A marriage takes place. Our soul is wedded to the soul of the natural object. And at the very moment of wedding Beauty is born. It springs from Love, just as Love itself originally sprang from the wedding of primitive man and woman.

In this process all will depend upon the mood. If we are not in the mood for it, we are unreceptive of Nature's impressions, and we are irresponsive. We do not come into touch with Nature. Consequently we see no Beauty. But if we are in a sensitive and receptive mood, if our minds are not preoccupied, and if our soul is open to the impressions which Nature is ever raining on it, then we respond to Nature's appeal. We feel ourselves in tune with her. We come into communion with her, and we see Beauty.

If we are ourselves feeling sad and sorrowful when we look out on Nature, and there all should happen to be bright and gay, we shall feel out of harmony with Nature, we shall not feel in touch with her, and we shall not see Beauty.

On the other hand, when we are in a glad and overflowing mood we shall be extraordinarily responsive to Nature's appeal, and see Beauty in a rugged, leafless oak tree or a poor old woman at the corner of some mean street. And if when we are in such a mood Nature happens to be at her best and brightest, as on some spring morning, the Beauty we shall then see will be overpowering, and we shall scarcely be able to contain ourselves for ecstasy of joy.

We shall have discovered an identity between what is in Nature and what is in us. In looking on Nature, we shall have been introduced into a Presence, greater than ourselves but like ourselves, which stirs in us this which we feel. When we see Beauty in Nature we are discovering that Nature is not merely a body, but *has* or *is* a soul. And the joy we feel is produced by the satisfaction our soul feels in coming into touch and harmony with this soul of Nature. Our soul is recognising samenesses between what is in it and what is in the soul of Nature, and feels joy in the recognition.

And the instinct of fellowship with our kind impels us to communicate to others what we ourselves have felt. We want to tell others what we have seen and what we have experienced.

We long, too, to share the joy which others also must have felt in contemplating Nature. We want especially to know and feel what those with far more sensitive souls than our own—the great poets, painters, and musicians—have felt. So we communicate our feelings to others; and we communicate with others, either personally or through their books or pictures or music, so that we may find out from them what more to look for, and may know better how to look for it. By so doing, our souls become more sensitive to the impressions of Nature, and we are better able to express those impressions. Our power of vision increases. Our soul's eye acquires a keener insight and sees deeper into the soul of Nature. We are able to enter more into the spirit of Nature, and the spirit of Nature is able to enter more into us. We arrive at a completer understanding between ourselves and Nature, are more in harmony with her, and consequently see more Beauty.

We see, indeed, what Nature really is. We see the reality behind the appearance—the content within the outward form. We are not for the moment concerned with the *cause* but with the *character* of Nature. We see the "I" behind the outward manifestation and representation. And if we have sympathy and understanding enough and are able truly to enter into the soul of Nature, we shall see the real "I" behind the common everyday "I"—just as the few who intimately know some great man see the real man behind the man who appears in the public eye—the real Beaconsfield or Kitchener behind the Beaconsfield or Kitchener of the daily press. And, as we see more of this real "I" in Nature and are better able to get in touch and harmony with her, so shall we see greater Beauty in Nature.

If we have petty, meagre souls we shall find little in common with the great soul of Nature, and consequently see only shallow Beauty. If we have great souls we shall have more in common and see more Beauty. But to arrive at a full understanding of the real Nature we must observe her from every point of view and see her in all her aspects. Only so shall we be able to understand her real self and see her full Beauty. And her aspects and the points of view from which we may observe them change so incessantly that the greatest of us falters. The more we see of Nature, the more we find there is to understand. And the more we understand Nature and commune with her, the more Beauty do we find there is to see. So to arrive at a complete understanding of Nature and see all her Beauty is beyond the capacity of us finite men.

Yet we are impelled to go on striving to see all we can. And in the following pages an attempt is made to show how, more Beauty in Nature may be discovered.

Often in the Himalaya I have watched an eagle circling overhead. I have sat on the mountain-side and watched it sail majestically along in graceful curves and circles, and with perfect ease and poise. Far above the earth it would range, and seemingly without exertion glide easily over tracts that we poor men could only enter by prodigious effort. Captivated by its grace of motion, and jealous of its freedom, I would for hours watch it. And this eagle I knew, from the height and distance from which it would swoop down on its prey, to be possessed of eyesight of unrivalled keenness in addition to its capacity for movement.

So this bird had opportunities such as no human being—not even an airman—has of seeing the earth and what is on it. At will it could glide over the loftiest mountain ranges. At will it could sail above the loveliest valleys. At will it could perch upon any chosen point and observe things at close range. In a single day this one eagle might have seen the finest natural scenery in the world—the highest mountain, the most varied forest, thickly populated plains and bare, open plains, peoples, animals, birds, insects, trees, flowers, all of the most varied description. In one day, and in the ordinary course of its customary circlings and sailings, it might have seen what men come from the ends of the Earth to view, and are content if they see only a hundredth part of what the eagle sees every day.

From its mountain eerie in Upper Sikkim it might have seen the rose of dawn flushing the snowy summits of Kinchinjunga, and far away Mount Everest. And soaring aloft, the eagle might have looked out over the populous plains of India and seen, like silver streaks, the rivers flowing down from the Himalaya to join in the far distance the mighty Mother Ganges. Then its eye might have ranged over the vast forest which clothes in dense green mantle the plain at the foot of the mountains from Nepal to Bhutan and Assam, and from the plain spreads up on the mountain-sides themselves and reaches to the very borders of eternal snow. Over this vast forest with its treasures of tree and plant, animal and insect life, tropical, temperate, and alpine, the eagle might have soared; and then, passing over the Himalayan watershed, have looked down upon the treeless, open, undulating, almost uninhabited plain of Tibet, and in the distance seen the great Brahmaputra River, which, circling round Bhutan, cuts clean through the Himalaya and, turning westward, also joins the Ganges.

In the whole world no more wonderful natural scenery is to be found. And the eagle with no unusual effort could see it all in a single day, and see it with a distinctness of sight no man could equal. But keen though its eyesight was and wide though its range, the eagle in all that beautiful region would see not a single beauty. Neither in the sunrise, nor in the snowy mountains, nor in the luxuriant tropical forest, nor in the flowers, the birds, the butterflies, nor in the people and animals, nor in the cataracts and precipices would it see any beauty whatever. The mountain would be to it a mere outline, the forests a patch of green, the rivers streaks of white, the animals just possible items of food. The eagle would see much, but it would see no beauty.

Perhaps we shall understand why it is that the eagle with these unbounded opportunities sees no beauty if we consider the case of a little midge buzzing round a man's body. The midge is roughly in about the same relation to the body of a man that the eagle is to the body of the Earth. The midge in its hoverings sees vast tracts of the human body; sees the features—the nose, the eye, the mouth; sees the trunk and the limbs and the head. But even in the most beautiful of men it would see no beauty. And it would see no beauty because it would have no soul to understand expression. It might be hovering round the features of a man when the smile on his lips and the exaltation in his eyes were expressive of the highest ecstasy of soul, but the midge would see no beauty in those features because it had not the soul to enter into the soul of the man and understand the expression on his face. All the little shades and gradations and tones and lights in the features of the man would be quite meaningless to the midge because it would know nothing of the man's soul, of which the features and the changes and variations in them were the outward manifestation. The midge would know nothing of the reality of the man which lay hidden behind the appearance.

It is the same with the eagle in respect to natural features as it is with the midge in respect to the features of the man. The eagle sees only the bare outward appearance of Nature, and sees no meaning in her features. It has no soul to enter into the soul of Nature and understand what the natural features are expressing. The delicate lights and shades and changes on the face of Nature have no meaning for it. It sees the bare appearance. It sees nothing of the reality behind the appearance. It has no soul to wed to the soul of Nature. It therefore sees no beauty.

But now supposing that among all the midges that buzz about a man there happened to be an artist-midge with exceeding sensitiveness of soul, one which was able to recognise a fundamental identity of life between it and the man, one which was able to recognise samenesses of feelings and emotions and aspirations, and by recognition of the samenesses between it and the man enter into the very life and soul of the man, then that midge would be able to understand all the varying expressions on the face of the man, and by understanding those expressions see their beauty.

We cannot expect an eagle in a similar way to have that sensitiveness of soul which would enable it to enter into the soul of Nature, understand Nature, and so see its Beauty. But what we cannot expect of the eagle we can expect of man. We can expect an Artist to appear who will be to the Earth what the artist-midge was to the man.

Man does to some extent enter into the soul of Nature. He has *some* understanding of Nature. He sees Beauty; and whenever he sees Beauty in Nature he is in touch with the soul of Nature. Even ordinary men see some of the Beauty of Nature and have some feeling of kinship with her. They have something in common between their soul and the soul of Nature. They have the sense of more in common between them and Nature than a midge has between it and a man.

And in a delicately sensitive man such as an artist—painter, poet, or musician—this sense of kinship with Nature is highly developed. In regard to his relationship with Nature he is like the finely sensitive and cultured artist-midge would be in regard to a man—the midge who, through understanding the inner soul and character of the man, was able to read the expression on his features and see their beauty.

What we ordinary men have to do, and what we especially want those gifted with unusually sensitive souls to do, is to bear in mind the difficulties which the midge has in understanding us and in seeing any beauty in us, and the way in which it would have to train and cultivate its faculties before it could ever hope to understand the expression on our features—to bear this in mind, and then to take ourselves in hand and develop the soul within us till it is fine enough and great enough to enter into the great soul of Nature.

The sense of Beauty we all possess in some slight degree is in itself a proof that behind the outward appearance of Nature there is a spiritual reality— an "I"—just as behind the outward appearance of the man which the artist-midge sees there is the "I" of the man. And by cultivating this sense—that is, by training and developing our capacity to see deeper into the heart of Nature, see more significance and meaning in each shade and change of her features, and read more understandingly what is going on deep within her soul—we shall enable ourselves to see a fuller and richer Natural Beauty.

So we look forward to the appearance among us of a great Artist who, born with an exceptionally sensitive soul, will deliberately heighten and intensify this sensitiveness, learn what others have experienced, compare notes with them, and train himself to detect the significance of every slightest indication which Nature gives of the workings of the soul within her; and then, recognising the sameness between his own feelings and the feelings of Nature, will fall deeply in love with her, give himself up utterly to her, marry her, and in their marriage give birth to Beauty of surpassing richness and intensity.

What we await, then, is an Artist with a soul worthy of being wedded to Nature. Puny, shallow artists will not be able to see much more of Nature than a midge sees of a man. What we want is a man with the physique, the abounding health and spirits, the fine intellect, the poetic power and imagination, the love of animals and his fellow-men, the skill, fitness, and gay courage of a Julian Grenfell. We want a man with the opportunities he had of mixing from childhood in London and in country houses with every grade and condition of men, with statesmen, soldiers, men of art, hunting men, racing men, schoolboys, undergraduates, literary men, gamekeepers, old family retainers—every kind and sort of human being. We want a man of such qualifications combined with the qualifications of a Darwin—with his love of natural history, his power of close and accurate observation, his genius for drawing right inferences from what he observed, his wide knowledge of Nature in her many manifestations, his sympathetic touch with every plant and animal, and his warm, affectionate nature in all human intercourse.

We want, in fact, a Naturalist-Artist—a combination of Julian Grenfell and Darwin. And this is no outrageously impossible, but a very likely and fitting combination. For Julian Grenfell wrote great poetry even in the trenches in Flanders between the two battles of Ypres. And with his love of country life, shooting, fishing, and hunting, his inclination might very easily have been directed towards natural history. If it had been and the opportunity had offered, we might have had the very type of Naturalist-Artist we are now awaiting. He would have had the physical fitness and capacity to endure hardships which are required for travel in parts of the Earth where the Natural Beauty is finest, and he would have had, too, the sensitiveness of soul to receive impressions and the power of expressing himself so that others might share with him the impressions he had felt. If after passing through the earlier stages of shooting and hunting birds and animals he had come to the more profitable stage of observing them, and had devoted to the observation of their habits and ways of life the same skill and acumen which he had shown in hunting them, he might, with his innate and genuine love of animals, very well have become a great naturalist as well as what he was—a great sportsman and a writer of great poetry.

It is for the advent of such Naturalist-Artist that we wait. But we have to prepare the way for him and do our share in helping to produce him. And this will now be my endeavour, for it so happens that I have been blessed with opportunities—some of my own making, some provided for me—of seeing Nature on a larger scale and under more varied aspects than falls to the lot of most men. I am ashamed when I reflect how little use I have made of those opportunities—how little I was prepared and trained to make the most of them. But this at least I can do: I can point out to the coming Artist those parts of the world where he is likely to see the Beauty of Nature most fully, and in greatest variety.

With this end in view I shall begin with the Sikkim Himalaya, over which the eagle flew, because it contains within a small area a veritable compendium of Nature. Rising directly out of the plains of India, practically within the tropics, these mountains rise far above the limits of perpetual snow. Their base is covered with luxuriant vegetation of a truly tropical character, and this vegetation extends through all the ranges from tropical to temperate and arctic. The animal, bird, and insect life does the same. And here also are to be found representative men of every clime. Similarly does the natural scenery vary from plain to highest mountain. There are roaring torrents and wide, placid rivers. The Sikkim Himalaya, looking down on the plains of India on the one side and the steppes of Tibet on the other, is the most suitable place I know for a study of Natural Beauty.

But there are beauties in Kashmir and in the great Karakoram Mountains behind Kashmir which are not found in Sikkim. And there are beauties in the Desert which are not found in either Sikkim or Kashmir. So I must take the Artist to these regions also.

And I choose Sikkim and Kashmir because these are easily accessible regions to which men with a thirst for Beauty can return again and again, till they are saturated with the atmosphere and have imbibed the true spirit of the region—till they have realised how much these natural features express sentiments which they, too, are wanting to express—their aspirations for the highest and purest, their longing for repose, their delight in warmth and affection, or whatever their sentiment might be. Thousands of Englishmen, cultured Indians, and travellers from all over the world, visit the Himalaya every year—some for sport, some for health, some for social enjoyment. Amongst these may be our Naturalist-Artist who year after year, drawn to Sikkim and Kashmir by his love of Natural Beauty, would learn to know Nature in the wonderfully varied aspects under which she is to be seen in those favoured regions, who would come into ever-deepening communion with her, would yearly see more Beauty in her, and would communicate to us the enjoyment he had felt.

But Natural Beauty includes within its scope a great deal more than only natural scenery. It includes the beauty of all natural objects—men and women as well as mountains, animals, and plants. So these also the Artist will have to keep within his purview. And his love of Nature, and consequently his capacity for seeing Natural Beauty, will be all the surer if he uses his head as well as his heart in forming his final conception of her—that is to say, his final for the moment, as no man ever has or *can* come to a literally final conception of Nature. So the Artist will pause now and then to test his view of Nature in the light of pure reason. For he will be well enough aware that neither Love nor Beauty can be perfect unless it be irradiated with Truth, and the three he will ever strive to keep together.

PART I

CHAPTER I.
THE SIKKIM HIMALAYA

The Sikkim Himalaya is a region first brought prominently into notice by the writings of Sir Joseph Hooker, the great naturalist, who visited it in 1848. It lies immediately to the east of Nepal, and can now be reached by a railway which ascends the outer range to Darjiling. It is drained by the Teesta River, up the main valley of which a railway runs for a short distance. The region is therefore easily accessible. For the purposes of this book it may be taken to include the flat open forest and grass-covered tract known as the Terai, immediately at the base of the mountain. This is only a few hundreds of feet above sea-level, so that from there to the summit of the Himalaya there is a rise of nearly 28,000 feet in about seventy miles. The lower part is in the 26th degree of latitude, so that the heat is tropical. And as the region comes within the sweep of the monsoon from the Bay of Bengal, there is not only great heat in the plains and lower valleys, but great moisture as well. The mountain-sides are in consequence clothed with a luxuriant vegetation.

To enter this wonderful region the traveller has first to cross the Ganges—the sacred river of the Hindus. Great rivers have about them a fascination all their own. They produce in us a sense of everlastingness and irresistibility. The Ganges, more than a mile wide, comes sweeping along in deep majestic flood from the far distance to the far distance, on and on unendingly, from all time to all time, and in such depth and volume that nothing human can withstand it. In the dry season, when it is low and the sun is shining, it is placid and benign with a bright and smiling countenance. Stately temples, set amidst sacred groves and graceful palms, lighten the banks. On the broad steps of the bathing ghats are assembled crowds of pious worshippers in clothes of every brilliant hue. The river has an aspect of kindliness and geniality and life-givingness. Its waters and rich silt have brought plenty to many a barren acre, and the dwellers on its banks know well that it issues from the holy Himalaya.

But the Ganges is not always in this gracious mood, and does not always wear this kindly aspect. In the rainy season it is a thing of terror. Overhead black, thundery clouds sweep on for days and weeks together towards the mountains. There is not a glimpse of sun. The rain descends as a deluge. The river is still further swollen by the melting of the snow on the Himalaya, and now comes swirling along in dark and angry mood, rising higher and higher in its banks, eating into them, and threatening to overtop them and carry death and destruction far and wide. Men no longer go down to meet it. They shrink back from it. They uneasily watch it till the fulness of its strength is spent and it has returned to its normal beneficent aspect.

No wonder such a river is regarded as sacred. To the more primitive people it is literally a living person—and a person who may be propitiated, a person who may do them harm if they annoy him, and do them good if they make themselves agreeable to him and furnish him with what he wants. To the cultured Hindus it is an object of the deepest reverence. If they can bathe in its waters their sins are washed away. If after death their ashes can be cast on its broad bosom, they will be secure of everlasting bliss. From perhaps the earliest days of our race, for some hundreds of thousands of years, men may have lived upon its banks. For it was in the forests beside great rivers, in a warm and even climate, that primitive men must have lived. They would have launched their canoes upon its waters, and used it as their only pathway of communication with one another. And always they would have looked upon it with mingled awe and affection. Besides the sun it would have been the one great natural object which would attract their attention. Insensibly the sight of that ever-rolling flood must have deeply affected them. They must have come to love it as they beheld it through the greater part of the year. The sight of its destructive power may have made them recoil for a time in fear and awe. But this would be forgotten as the flood subsided, and the river was again smooth and smiling and passing peacefully along before them.

So men do not run away from it. They gather to it. They build great cities on its banks, and come from great distances to see it. They perform pilgrimages every year in thousands to the spot where it issues from the Himalaya. And they penetrate even to its source far back and high up in the mountains.

To the most enlightened, also, the Ganges should be an object of reverence for its antiquity, for its future, and for its power. From the surface of the Bay of Bengal the sun's rays have drawn particles of water into the atmosphere. Currents in the air have carried them for hundreds of miles over the sea and over the plains of Bengal, till the chill of the Himalaya Mountains has caused them to condense and fall in snow and rain. But some have been carried farther. They have been transported right over the Himalaya at a height of at least 20,000 feet, till they have finally fallen in Tibet. It is a striking fact that some of the water in the Ganges is from rivers in Tibet which have cut their way clean through the mighty range of the Himalaya. The Arun River, for example, rises in Tibet and cuts through the Himalaya by a deep gorge in the region between Mount Everest and Kinchinjunga. These rivers are, indeed, much older than the mountains. They were running their course before the Himalaya were upheaved, and they kept wearing out a channel for themselves as the mountains rose and slowly over-towered them.

Reverence, therefore, is due to the Ganges on account of its vast antiquity. Reverence also is due because it will flow on like now for hundreds of thousands and perhaps for millions of years to come. Round and round in never-ceasing cycle the water is drawn up from the ocean, is carried along in the clouds, descends upon the mountains, and gathers in the Ganges to flow once more into the sea. The Ganges may gradually change its course as it eats into first one bank and then the other. But it will flow on and on and on for as far into the future as the human eye can ken.

And its power, so terrifying to primitive man—even to us at times—will become more and more a power for good. Already great canals have been taken from its main stream and its tributaries, and millions of acres have been irrigated by its water, thus helping to bring to birth great crops of wheat and rice, cotton, sugar-cane, and oil-seeds. Schemes for utilising the water-power in its fall through the mountains by converting it into electric power are in contemplation, so that railways may be run by it and power for great industries be furnished. Once more, too, the course of the river may become a line of communication as sea-planes are used to fly from town to town and alight upon its surface.

So as we come to know the river in its deepest significance, our impression of its everlastingness and its irresistible power remains. But our sense of fear diminishes. We feel that the river is ready to co-operate with us. That it is capable of being taken in hand and led. That its power is not essentially destructive but beneficent. That there is in it almost inexhaustible capacity for helping plant and beast and man. And that it is a friend and anxious to help us.

The Hindus have been right all along in worshipping it. Their worship, with tropical luxuriance, may have developed to extravagant lengths. But the instinct which promoted this worship was perfectly sound. The river bears within its breast great life-giving properties, and in worshipping the river the Hindus were half-consciously expressing their sense of dependence on these life-giving properties, and of affection and gratitude to the river for the benefits it conferred. Mere fear of its destructive character—fear alone—

would not produce the desire for worship. They did and do fear the river, but behind the fear is a feeling that it *can* be propitiated, that it *can* be induced to help man and does not want to thwart him. And here they were perfectly right. We are at last learning the way by which this may be done, and now see clearly what the Hindus only vaguely felt, that the heart of the river is right enough—that once it is tamed and trained it can bring untold good to man.

This the Artist will readily discern. He will enter into the spirit of the river. He will read its true character. Refusing to be terrorised by its more tremendous moods, he will exult in its might, and see in it a potent agency for good. In these ways the river will make its appeal to him; and responding to the appeal, the Artist will see great Beauty in the river and describe that Beauty to us.

* * *

Beyond the river, before we reach the mountain, we have to pass over absolutely level cultivated plains, without a single eminence in sight. To most they would appear dull, monotonous, uninteresting. There is no horizon to which the eye can wander and find satisfaction in remote distance. There is no hill to which to raise our eyes and our souls with them. The outlook is confined within the narrowest limits. Palm trees, banyan trees, houses, walled gardens, everywhere restrict it. The fields are small, the trees and houses numerous. Nothing distant is to be seen. To the European the prospect is depressing. But to the Bengali it is his very life. These densely inhabited plains are his home. They have, therefore, all the attraction which familiar scenes in which men have grown up from childhood always have. A Bengali prefers them to high mountains. He loves the sight of the brilliant emerald rice-fields, of the tall feathery palms, of the shady banyan trees, of the flaming poinsettias, the bright marigolds, cannas and bougainvillea, the many-coloured crotons and calladiums, the sweet-scented jasmine, oranges, tuberoses, and gardenia; and the gaudy jays, the swiftly darting parrots, and the playful squirrels. He loves, too, the bathing-pools, and the patient oxen, and the cool, sequestered gardens. And he loves these things for their very nearness. His attention is not distracted to distant horizons and inaccessible heights. All is close to the eye and easily visible. His world may be small, but it is all within reach. He can know well each tree and flower, each bird and animal. It is not a wide and varied life. But it is an intense and very vivid life; and to the Bengali, on that account, more preferable. And if it is confined it is at least confined in the open air, and in a climate of perpetual summer.

* * *

Beyond this highly cultivated and thickly populated part, and still in the plains, we come to a wild jungle country which stretches up to the foothills, and is swampy, pestilential, and swarming with every kind of biting insect. It is a nasty country to travel through. But it has its interests. There grow here remarkable grasses, with tall straight shoots gracefully bending over at the top from the weight of their feathery heads; and so high are these gigantic grasses that they often reach above the head of a man on an elephant. The areas covered by them are practically impenetrable to men on foot, and there is a mysterious feel about this region, for it is the haunt of rhinoceros, tigers, and boars. In passing through it we have an uneasy feeling that almost anything may appear on the instant, and that once we were on foot and away from the path we would be irretrievably lost—drowned in a sea of waving grass.

From this sea of grass rise patches of forest and single trees. The most prevalent is the Sal tree *(Shorea robusta)*, a magnificent gregarious tree with a tall straight stem and thick glossy foliage. But the most conspicuous in March and April is the Dák tree *(Butea frondosa)*, an ungainly tree, but remarkable for its deep rich scarlet flowers, like gigantic sweet-peas but of a thick velvety texture. These flowers blossom before the leaves appear, and when the tree is in full bloom it looks like a veritable flame in the forest.

Another beautiful tree which is found in this lower part is the *Acacia catechu*, known in Northern India as the Khair tree, and found all about the foothills of the Himalaya. Not tall and stately, but rather contorted and ample like the oak, it has a graceful feathery foliage and a kindly inviting nature.

* * *

Proceeding over these level plains, which as we approach the mountains are covered with dense forest, stagnant morasses, and trim tea-gardens, we one morning awake to find that over the horizon to the north hangs a long cloud-like strip, white suffused with pink—level on its lower edge but with the upper edge irregular in outline. No one who had not seen snow mountains before would suppose for a moment that that strip could be a line of mountain summits. For there is not a trace of any connection with the earth. Between it and the earth is nothing but blue haze. And it is so high above the horizon that it seems incredible that any such connection could exist. Yet no one who *had* seen snow mountains could doubt for an instant that that rose-flushed strip of white was the Himalaya. For it possesses two unmistakable characteristics which distinguish it from any cloud. Firstly, the lower edge is absolutely straight and horizontal: it is exactly parallel with the horizon. Secondly, the upper edge is jagged, and the outline of the jaggedness cuts clean and perfectly defined against the intense blue of the sky.

No one who knows mountains could doubt that this line was the Himalaya, yet every time we see it afresh we marvel more. We know for certain that

The Heart Of Nature Or The Quest For Natural Beauty | 19

those sharp edges *are* the summits of mountains whose base is on this solid earth. Yet, however sure we may be of that fact, we do not cease to wonder. And as we gaze upon that line of snowy summits no more—indeed, less—intrinsically beautiful than many a cloud, yet unspeakably more significant, we are curiously elated. Something in us leaps to meet the mountains. And we cannot keep our eyes away. We seem lifted up, and feel higher possibilities within ourselves and within the world than we had ever known before. As we travel onward we strain to keep the mountains continually in sight, for we cannot bear to leave them. We feel better men for having seen them, and for the remainder of our days we would keep them in continuing remembrance.

* * *

As we come closer under the mountains the base emerges from the haze and the line of snowy peaks disappears behind the nearer outer ranges. Then we come to these ranges themselves, which rise with considerable abruptness out of the level plains with very little intermediate modulation of form, and we find them densely clothed in forest—true, rich, luxuriant, tropical forest with all the delights of glistening foliage, graceful ferns and palms, glorious orchids, and brilliant butterflies.

CHAPTER II.
THE TEESTA VALLEY

This great forest, which extends for hundreds of miles along the slopes of the Himalaya, reaches up from the plains to the snows. In the lower part it is a truly tropical forest, and about a tropical forest there is something peculiarly mysterious. A strange stillness is over all. Not, indeed, the absolute silence of the desert, where literally not a sound is heard; for here in the forest, even during the hot noonday quiet, there is always the purring of insect life. But that stillness when not a leaf moves and no harsh noise is heard, when an impressive hush is laid upon the scene and we seem to be in some mysterious Presence dominating all about us and rousing our expectancy.

A kind of awe seizes us, and with it also comes a keen exhilaration. We can see at most for a hundred yards in any direction. But we know that the forest extends like this for hundreds of miles. And we realise that if we wandered off the track we might never find it again. It is all very awe-inspiring, and in some ways frightening. Still, we are thrilled by the sight of such a profusion, intensity, and variety of life. In this hot, steamy atmosphere plants and trees grow in luxuriant abundance. Every inch of soil is occupied. And these forests are not like woods in England, which contain only three or four species—oaks, beeches, sycamores, etc. In these Sikkim forests we seldom see two trees of the same kind standing next each other. One tree may be more prevalent than others, but there is always great variety in the forms and colours of the stems, the branches, the leaves, the flowers, the habit of growth. There are trees of immense height with tall, strong, straight stems, and there are shrubs like hydrangeas of every size and description. There are climbers as huge as cables. And there are gentle little plants hardly rising above the ground. There is no end to the variety of plant life, and we have an inner spring of delight as we come across treasure after treasure that hitherto we had only seen reared with infinite care in some expensive hot-house.

And what we see is only, we feel, a stray sample of what there is to be seen. What may there not be in those forest depths which we dare not enter for fear of losing our way! What other towering forest monarchs might we not come across if we plunged into the forest! What other exquisite flowers, what insects, what birds, what animals! What wealth of insect life may there not be at the tops of the trees where the fierce sunshine hidden from us by their leaves is drawing out their flowers! What may there not be going on in the ground beneath us! We know, that in these forests, perhaps near enough to see us, though their forms are hidden by their likeness to their leafy surroundings and the dappled sunlight, are animals as various as elephants, tigers, leopards, foxes, squirrels, and bats; birds as various as hawks, parrots, and finches; and insects from butterflies, bees, and wasps to crickets, beetles, and ants. The forest, we know, in addition to all the wealth of tree and plant life, is teeming with animal and insect life, though of this we are able to see very little, so carefully do animals conceal themselves. In the night they emerge, and in the morning and evening there is a deafening din of insect life. But at noonday there is a soft and solemn hush, and we are tense with curiosity to know all that is going on in those mysterious forest depths and up among the tree-tops, so close but so impossible of access.

The great forest is the very epitome of life. Concentrated here in small compass is every form and variety of living thing, from lowliest plant to forest monarch, from simplest animalcule to elephant, monkey, and man. There is life and abundant life all about us. But it is not the noisy, clamorous, obtrusive life of the city. It is a still, intense life, full of untold possibilities for good or harm. And herein lies its mystery: we see much, but we feel that there is infinitely more behind.

Of this life of the forest in all its richness, intensity, and variety we shall come to know more as we ascend the Teesta Valley till it reaches the snows, and tropical plant and animal life changes first to temperate and then to arctic forms. But first we must note some beauties of the valley itself.

* * *

The valley of the great Teesta River, the valleys of its tributaries, the gorges through which the main river and its tributaries rush, the cascades pouring in succession down the mountain-sides, the sequestered glens and dells—all these have beauties which the terrific rain and the mists in which they are usually enveloped do not hide but augment.

The River Teesta itself, though only a minor contributor to the Brahmaputra, is nevertheless during the rainy season, when it is fed both by the falling rain and by the melting snows and glaciers of the Kinchinjunga region, impressive in its might and energy. With a force and tumult that nothing could withstand it comes swirling down the valley. Before its rushing impetuosity everything would be swept away. For it is no little tossing torrent: it possesses depth and weight and volume, and sweeps majestically along in great waves and cataracts. In comparison with the serene composure of the lofty summits here is life and force and activity to the full—and destructive activity at that, to all appearance. Yet as, from the safety of a bridge by which the genius of man has spanned it, we look upon the turmoil, a strange thrill comes through us. There is such splendid energy in the river. We are fascinated by the power it displays. It is glorious to look upon. Alarming in a way it is. But we know it can only act within certain strictly defined bounds. A foot beyond those bounds it is powerless. And while it is already confined by Nature within these limits, we know the day will come when it will be completely within the control of man and its very power available for our own purposes. So in the end it is with no sense of terror that we watch the raging river in its headlong course. Rather do we enjoy the sight of such exultant energy, which will one day be at man's disposal. We rejoice with the river in a feeling of power, and herein lies its Beauty for us.

* * *

As we look at the tremendous gorges through which the river clears its way we again are filled with awe and wonder. Straight facing us is a clean, sheer cliff of hardest, sternest rock. It cannot be actually perpendicular, but to all appearance it is. And the mere sight of it strengthens our souls. Here is granite solidity, and yet no mere stolid obstinacy. For these cliffs have risen— so the geologists tell us—through their own internal energy to their present proud position. They have, indeed, had to give place to the river to this extent that they have had to acknowledge his previous right of way and to leave a passage for him in their upward effort. The river is careful to exact that much toll from them year by year. But having paid that toll, they have risen by a process of steady, long persistence, and have maintained themselves in their exalted position by sheer firmness and tenacity of character. And as, dripping with warm moisture and carrying with them in any available crevice graceful ferns and trees, they rise above us high up into the clouds, and form the buttresses of those snowy peaks of which we catch occasional glimpses, we are impressed not only with the height of the aspiration those peaks embody, but with the strength and persistency of purpose which was necessary to carry the aspiration into effect.

Overpowered, indeed, we feel at times—shut in and overshadowed by what seems so infinitely greater than ourselves. The roaring river fills the centre of the gorge. The precipitous cliffs rise sheer on either hand. We seem for the moment too minute to cope with such titanic conditions. But sometimes by circumventing the cliffs and after a long tedious detour appearing high above them, sometimes by blasting a passage across their very face, we have proved ourselves able to overcome them. They no longer affright us. And as we return down the valley after a journey to its upmost limit, it is with nothing but sheer delight that we look upon these cliffs. They simply impress us with the strength that must go along with elevation of purpose if that purpose is to be achieved. Unbuttressed by these staunch cliffs the mountains could never have reached their present height. We glory, then, with the cliffs in their solidity and strength as they proudly face the world. And we recognise that in this firmness and consistency of purpose lies their especial Beauty.

* * *

In contrast with the swirling river and hard, rugged cliffs we, quite close to them, and hidden away in a modest tributary of a tributary in the quiet forest depths, will happen upon some deep sequestered pool which imbues us with a sense of the delicacy and reserve of Nature. We here see her in a peculiarly tender aspect. The pool is still and clear. The lulling murmurs of a waterfall show whence it draws its being. A gentle rivulet carries the overbrim away. It is bounded by rocks and boulders green with exquisite ferns and mosses. Overhanging it are weeping palms with long straight leaves. Trees, with erect stems as tall as Nelson's Column, strain upward to the light. Butterflies in numbers flutter noiselessly about. The air is absolutely still and of a feel like satin. Clouds of intangible softness and clean and white as snow float around, appear, dissolve, and reappear. Through the parting in the overhanging trees the intense blue sky is seen in glimpses. The sun here and there pierces through the arching foliage, and the greens of the foliage glisten brighter still. The whole atmosphere of the spot is one of reticence and reserve. Yet quiet though it be and restful though it be, there is no sense of stagnation. The pool, though deep and still, is vividly alive. Its waters are continually being renewed. And the forest, though not a leaf moves, is, we know, straining with all the energy of life for food and light, for air and moisture. So by this jewel of a pool in its verdant setting we have a sense of an activity which is gentle and refined. The glen's is a shy and intimate Beauty, especially congenial to us after the forceful Beauty of the river and the bold, proud Beauty of the cliffs. But it is no insipid Beauty: in its very quietness and confidence is strength.

CHAPTER III.
THE FOREST

The Teesta Valley in its lowest part is only 700 feet above sea-level. It is deep and confined and saturated with perpetual moisture. Hardly a breath of wind stirs, and all plant life is forced as in a hothouse. The trees do not, indeed, grow as high as the Big Trees of California or the eucalyptus in Australia, but some of these in the Teesta Valley are 200 feet in height with buttressed trunks between 40 and 50 feet in girth, and give the same impression of stateliness and calm composure. With incredible effort and incessant struggle they have attained their present proud position, and the traveller most willingly accords them the tribute that is their due.

Grand tropical oaks nearly 50 feet in girth also occur, screw-pines 50 feet in height with immense crowns of grassy leaves 4 feet long, palms of many kinds, rattan-canes, bamboos, plantains, and tall grasses such as only grow in dense, hot jungles. Gigantic climbers tackle the loftiest trees. One allied to the gourd bears immense yellowish-white pendulous blossoms; another bears curious pitcher-shaped flowers. Vines, peppers, and pothos interlace with the palms and plantains in impenetrable jungle. Orchids clothe the trees. Everywhere and always we hear the whirr and hum of insect life, sometimes soft and soothing, sometimes harsh and strident. And floating about wherever we look are butterflies innumerable, many dull and unpretentious, but some of a brilliancy of colour that makes us gasp with pleasure.

We may be pouring with perspiration, pestered by flies and mosquitoes, and in constant dread of leeches. But we forget all such annoyances in the joy of these wonders of the tropics, whether they be trees or orchids, ferns or butterflies. And to see one of these gorgeous insects alight in front of us, slowly raise and lower his wings and turn himself about almost as if he were showing himself off for our especial pleasure, compensates us for every worry his fellows in the insect world may cause us.

As might be expected, in the steamy, dripping atmosphere ferns are a predominating feature in the vegetation. Not less than two hundred different kinds are found. The most noticeable are the tree ferns, of which alone there are eight species. Their average height is about 20 feet, but plants of 40 and

50 feet are not uncommon. And with their tall trunks and crown of immense graceful fronds they form a striking feature in the forest, and in the moister valleys where they attain their full luxuriance they may be seen in extensive groves as well as in little groups. Four kinds of maidenhair, always light and graceful and attractive, are found; and of ferns common to Europe, *Osmunda regalis*, the Royal fern of Europe, and the European moonwort and alder›s-tongue ferns. Then there is a fern which attains to gigantic proportions, especially in the cool forests, where its massive fronds grow to more than 5 yards in length and 3 in breadth, with a spread over all, measuring from tip to tip of opposite fronds, of 8 yards. One handsome climbing fern clothes the trunks of tall trees; another which climbs on grasses and the smaller shrubs is common; and another forms almost impenetrable thickets 15 or 20 feet high. Of the kinds which grow on rocks and trees the most delicately beautiful are the filmy ferns, of which there are eight kinds. The Irish filmy is the largest, covering the face of large rocks under dense shade, its fronds growing to over a foot in length. Many polypodiums and aspleniums grow gracefully on the rocks and trees during the rainy season. One especially elegant polypodium growing on the ground has fronds about 6 or 7 feet long, and sometimes as much as 20 feet, and of proportionate width. Another conspicuous fern is the bird's-nest fern with its large, massive fronds growing under shade on rocks and stems of trees.

Unless we are fern experts it is impossible for us to identify each among so many species. But, at any rate, we gather an impression of elegance and grace, often of airy lightness, and of wonderful variety of size and form.

* * *

From the ferns we look to the rest of the forest, and after the first bewilderment at the profusion and variety of vegetation we try to fasten on to a few individuals or types which we can identify as having seen elsewhere in some other part of India or in some palm-house in England. We are in the still, steamy atmosphere of a hot-house, and we are conscious that all round us, growing in luxuriant abundance, are rare and beautiful plants of which a single specimen would be treasured and treated with every fostering care in England. But we sigh to be able to recognise these treasures and make contact between home and this exceptionally favoured region—favoured, that is to say, as regards plant life. From among the giant trees, the bamboos, the palms, the climbers, the shrubs, the flowers, the orchids, we look out anxiously for friends—or at least for acquaintances whom we hope may develop into friends as we meet them again and again on our journeys through the forest.

Of the flowers, the orchids are naturally the first to attract us. They shine out as real gems in the greenery around them. The eye jumps to them at once.

Here seems to be something as nearly perfect in colour, form, and texture as it could possibly be. If the orchid is white it is of the purest whiteness, and shines chaste and unsullied amidst its dull surroundings. If it is purple, or pale yellow, or golden-yellow, or rose, or violet, or white, the colour has always a depth and purity which is deeply satisfying. And it seems to be because the waxy texture of these orchids is such a perfect medium for the display of colour that orchids are so exceptionally beautiful. The texture is of the very consistency best adapted for revealing the beauty of colour. And when we pluck a spray of these choice treasures from the forest branch and hold it in the sunlight, we feel we are seeing colour almost in perfection.

The colour and texture are beautiful enough in themselves. But an added attraction in these orchids is their form—the curvature of their sepals and petals, and the wonderful little pitchers and cups and lips and tongues which an orchid exhibits. And the form is no mere geometrical pattern of lines and curves. It is obviously an ingenious contrivance devised for some special purpose. That purpose we now know to be the attraction of insects, who in sucking the orchid's honey will unconsciously carry on their wings or backs the flower's pollen to fertilise another orchid. Though whether the insect in the long centuries by probing at the orchid has forced it to adapt itself to it, or whether the flower has forced the insect to adapt itself to the flower, or whether—as seems most likely—a process of mutual adaptation has been going on century by century, and the flower and insect have been gradually adapting themselves to one another, is still a matter of discussion among naturalists.

We cannot gather an orchid of any kind without marvelling at its intricate construction. And when we are looking at the orchid in its natural surroundings in the forest itself and see the enormous numbers and the immense variety, in size and form and habits, of the insects around the orchid, and think how the orchid has to select its own particular species of insect and cater for that, and the insect among all the flowers has to select the particular species of orchid; and how the insect, whether butterfly or bee or moth or gnat or ant, or any other of the numerous kinds of insect, and the orchid have to adapt themselves to each other—we see how marvellous the mutual adaptation of flower to insect and insect to flower must have been. We see how the particular species of orchid must have chosen the particular species of bee, and the particular species of bee that particular species of orchid, and the bee and orchid set themselves to adapt themselves to one another, the orchid using all the devices of colour, scent, sweetness of honey, to attract the insect, and gradually shaping itself so that the insect can better reach the honey, and the insect lengthening its proboscis and otherwise adapting itself so that it can better secure what it wants. And we see how perfectly—how nearly perfectly—the flower is designed for its purpose.

But what is perhaps most remarkable of all about an orchid is that this marvel of colour and form and of texture of fabric unfolds itself from within a most ungainly, unsightly, unlikely-looking tuber. From shapeless, colourless tubers, which attach themselves to trunks and branches of trees and cling on to rocks, there emerge these peerless aristocrats of the flower-world, finished, polished, immaculate, and reigning supreme through sheer distinction and excellence at every point—and also because theirs is clearly no ephemeral convolvulus-like beauty which will fade and vanish away in a twinkling, but is a beauty intensely matured, strong and deep and firm.

* * *

Of the 450 species of orchids found in the Sikkim Forest, many are very rare. But fortunately the rarest are not the most beautiful in colour and form. Some very beautiful orchids are also very common. The most common are the dendrobiums, of which there are about forty species. The finest and best known is the *Dendrobium nobile*. It grows in the lower hills and valleys up to 5,000 feet, and also in the plains. The flowers vary both in size and shade of colour; but in Sikkim the sepals and petals are always purple, shading off into white at the base. The tip has a central blotch of very deep purple surrounded by a broad margin of pale yellow or white. This orchid is now very common in English hot-houses, so here is one point of contact with the tropical forest.

The *D. densiflorum* is equally common and grows in much the same region. It flowers in a dense cluster on a stalk somewhat after the fashion of a hyacinth. The sepals and petals of this beautiful species are of a pale yellow, while the lip is of a rich orange. One of the most charming of the Sikkim dendrobiums has the smell of violets, and the sepals and petals are white-tipped with violet, the stem being sometimes 2 1/2 feet long. Another noteworthy dendrobium is the *D. pierardi*, whose prevailing colour is a beautiful rose or pale purple.

After the dendrobiums the coelogyne are the most worth noting. The *Coelogyne cristata* is common at elevations of from 5,000 to 8,000 feet, and flowers during March and April. It has numerous large flowers, which are pure white throughout, with the exception of the lamellae of the lip, which are yellow. It may be seen in flower in March in the orchid-house at Kew. In the forest it grows in such profusion as to make the trunk of a dead tree look as if it were covered with snow.

The *C. humilis* is known as the Himalayan crocus. It grows like a crocus from a pseudo-bulb at elevations from 7,000 to 8,500 feet, and flowers during

February and March. The flowers are white and from 2 to 2 1/2 inches in diameter. The lip is speckled with purple towards the edge.

Not so common but larger and handsomer than the dendrobiums are the cymbidiums, of which there are sixteen different species, usually with long grassy leaves and many-flowered drooping racemes with large handsome flowers. A very sweet-scented species is the *Cymbidium eburneum,* which is common between elevations of 1,000 to 3,000 feet, and flowers during March and April. The prevailing colour of the flowers is an ivory white, but the ridge on the lip is a brilliant yellow. This also may be seen at Kew in March.

These are some of the commonest orchids and all now grow in England, so that we can begin to get a footing in the forest and not feel that it is so completely strange to us. And as we ascend higher we shall find many more friends among the flowers. And to guide us among the trees and flowers we fortunately have Sir Joseph Hooker, who in his "Himalayan Journals" has described this botanist's paradise in loving detail, so we cannot do better than follow him. Amid the many plants he mentions we can only select a few, but these few will at least help to give us some conception of the whole and show the range of variation as we ascend.

As we proceed higher up the valley to an altitude of about 4,000 feet, European trees and plants begin to be intermingled with the tropical vegetation. Hornbeams appear, and birch, willow, alder, and walnut grow side by side with wild plantains, palms, and gigantic bamboos. Brambles, speedwells, forget-me-nots, and nettles grow mixed with figs, balsams, peppers, and huge climbing vines. The wild English strawberry is found on the ground, while above tropical orchids like the dendrobiums cover the trunks of the oaks. The bracken and the club-moss of our British moors grow associated with tree-ferns. And English grow alongside Himalayan mosses.

The valley itself continues of the same character—deep with its steep sides clothed in forest and the path scrambling over spurs, making wide detours up side valleys, or scraping along the sides of cliffs which stand perpendicularly over the raging river below. Only here and there are clearings in the forest where Lepchas or Nepalese have built themselves a few wooden houses and roughly cultivated the land. Otherwise we are under the same green mantle of forest which extends everywhere over the mountains; and though we are now piercing straight through the main axis of the Himalaya, we seldom catch even a glimpse of the snowy heights which must be so near.

But the vegetation is distinctly changing in character as we ascend—the most tropical trees and plants gradually disappearing, and more and more flowers of the temperate zone coming into evidence. And as we pierce farther into the mountains the climate becomes sensibly drier and the forest lighter.

There is still a heavy enough rainfall to satisfy any ordinary plant or human being. But there is not the same deluge that descends upon the outer ridges. So the forest is not so dense. Frequently in its place social grasses clothe the mountain-sides; and yellow violets, primulas, anemones, delphiniums, currants, and saxifrages remind us of regions more akin to our own.

Now, too, we have reached the habitat of the rhododendrons, which are so peculiarly a glory of Sikkim, and it is worth while to pause and take special note of them. Out of the thirty species which are found in Sikkim, all the most beautiful have been introduced—chiefly by Sir Joseph Hooker—into England, and are grown in many parks and gardens as well as at Kew. So English people can form some idea of what the flowering trees of the Sikkim Forest are like. But they must multiply by many times the few specimens they see in an English park or hot-house, and must realise that as cowslips are in a grassy meadow, so are these rhododendron trees in the Sikkim Forest. Red, mauve, white, or yellow, they grow as great flowers among the green giants of the forest and brighten it with colour. The separate blossoms of a rhododendron tree cannot compare in beauty with the individual orchid. There is in them neither the deep richness of colour nor wonder of form nor sense of deeply matured excellence. The claim of the rhododendron to favour is rather in the collective quantity and mass of flowers so that by sheer weight of numbers it can produce its effect of colour. In some of the upper valleys the mountain slopes are clothed in a deep green mantle glowing with bells of scarlet, white, or yellow.

Perhaps the most splendid of these rhododendrons is *Rhododendron grande* or *argenteum,* which grows to a height of from 30 to 40 feet, and has waxy bell-shaped flowers of a yellowish-white suffused with pink, 2 to 3 inches long and about the same across. The scarlet *R. arboreum,* so general in the Himalaya, is common in Sikkim and furnishes brilliant patches of colour in the forest. And a magnificent species is *R. Auchlandii* or *Griffithianum,* which has large white flowers tinged with pink, of a firm fleshy texture and with a mouth 5 inches across. It has been called the queen of all flowering shrubs. It grows well in Cornwall, and among the hybrids from it is the famous Pink Pearl.

R. Falconeri, a white-flowered species, is eminently characteristic of the genus in habit, place of growth and locality, never occurring below 10,000 feet. In foliage it is incomparably the finest. It throws out one or two trunks clean and smooth, 30 feet or so high, the branches terminated by immense leaves, deep green above edged with yellow and ruby red-brown below. The creamy white flowers are shaded with lilac and are slightly scented. They are produced in tightly-packed clusters 9 to 15 inches across and twenty or more in numbers.

A peculiar (in that it is of all the species the only one that is epiphytal) but much the largest flowered species is the *R. Dalhousiae*. It grows, like the orchids, among ferns and moss upon the trunks of, large trees, especially oaks and magnolias, and attains a height of 6 to 8 feet. The flowers are three to seven in a head, and are 3 1/2 to 5 inches long and as much across the mouth, white with an occasional tinge of rose and very fragrant. In size, colour, and fragrance of the blossoms this is the noblest of the genus. It grows out-of-doors in Cornwall and in the greenhouse in other parts of England as a scraggy bush 10 to 12 feet high. *R. barbatum* is a tree from 40 to 60 feet high, producing flowers of a rich scarlet or blood-colour, and sometimes puce or rich pink. It is one of the most beautiful of the Himalayan rhododendrons, and is now very common in England, growing freely out-of-doors. Another truly superb plant is *R. Maddeni,* with very handsome pure white flowers 3 1/2 to 4 inches long and as much across the mouth. This is now a special favourite in England. It grows in large bushes in the open in Cornwall and is very sweet-scented. *R. virgatum* is a beautiful delicately white-flowered shrub. And *R. campylo-carpum* displays masses of exquisite pale yellow bells of rarest delicacy.

Besides rhododendrons, ash, walnut, and maple become more abundant as we ascend, and at 9,000 feet larch appears, and there are woods of a spruce resembling the Norwegian spruce in general appearance. Among the plants are wood-sorrel, bramble, nut, spiraea, and various other South European and North American genera.

The climate is no longer stifling and the leeches have disappeared. We miss many beauties of the tropical forest. But, with the vegetation more and more resembling what we are accustomed to in Europe, we are feeling more at home. The path winds through cool and pleasant woods, following the varying contour of the mountain-sides. We are no longer oppressed by the strangeness of the life around us. At almost every turn we come across something new yet not wholly unfamiliar. And standing out especially in our memory of this region will be the sight of a gigantic lily rearing itself ten feet high in the forest, and as pure in its perfect whiteness as if it had been grown in a garden. It is the *Lilium giganteum,* and it has fourteen flowers on a single stalk and each 4 1/2 inches long and the same across.

We still love most of all the white violets we have as children picked in an English wood, and even this great white lily will never supplant them in our affections. But the sight of that glorious plant rising proudly from amidst the greenery of its forest setting will be for us more than any picture. And its being "wild" has the same fascination for us that a flower that is "wild," and not garden grown, has for a child. In a florist's shop we may see lilies even more beautiful than this, but the enjoyment we get from seeing the florist's production bears no comparison whatever with the enjoyment we get from seeing this lily in a distant Himalayan forest where not so many white men ever go. We often have experiences which perceptibly age us. But this is one of those experiences which most certainly make us younger. We are once again children finding flowers in a wood.

As we proceed upward the valley opens out, the mountains recede and are less steep. They are also less wooded, their slopes become more covered with grass, and the river, no longer a raging torrent, now meanders in a broad bed. The great peaks are somewhere close by, but we do not see the highest, and for the Himalaya the scenery is somewhat tame. But the number of herbaceous plants is great. A complete record of them would include most of the common genera of Europe and North America. Among them are purple, yellow, pink, and white primulas, golden potentillas, gentians of deepest azure, delicate anemones, speedwells, fritillaries, oxalis, balsams, and ranunculus. One special treasure of this part is a great red rose *(Rosa macrophylla)*, one of the most beautiful of Himalayan plants whose single blossoms are as large as the palm of the hand. With these plants from the temperate zone are mixed the far outliers of the tropical genera—orchids, begonias, and others—whose ascent to these high regions has been favoured by the great summer heat and moisture.

We are now in the region of the primulas for which (besides its orchids and rhododendrons) Sikkim is famous. Sikkim may indeed be called the headquarters of the Indian primroses, and many species are found there which appear to occur nowhere else. There are from thirty to forty species, the majority growing at altitudes from 12,000 to 15,000 feet, two or three only being found below 10,000 feet, and two or three as high as 16,000 to 17,000 feet. The best known is the *Primula sikkimensis*, which grows well in England and resembles a gigantic cowslip. It thrills us to see it growing in golden masses in the high valleys in wet boggy places—though the precise colour may be better described as lemon-yellow rather than gold.

The prevailing colour of the primulas is purple, but white, yellow, blue, and pink are also found. The *P. denticulata* has purple to bright sapphire blue flowers, and great stretches of country are almost blue with the lovely heads of this primrose. Miles of country can be seen literally covered with *P. obtusifolia*, which has purple flowers and a strong metallic smell. *P. Kingii* is a lovely plant with flowers of such a dark claret colour that they are almost black. And perhaps the most striking primula is *P. Elwesiana*, with large solitary deflexed purple flowers.

Poppies also are a feature of the Sikkim vegetation. Near the huts the people cultivate a majestic species near *Menconopsis simplicifolia*, but it grows in dense clusters 2 or 3 feet high. The flowers vary in diameter from 5 to 7 inches, and are an intensely vivid blue on opening, though they change before fading into purple. *M. simplicifolia* itself is also found at altitudes from 12,000 to 15,000 feet—a clear light blue species of special beauty, growing as a single flower on a single stem, and now to be seen at both Edinburgh and Kew. Another beautiful poppy is the *M. nepalensis*, which grows in the central dampest regions of Sikkim at elevations of 10,000 to 11,000 feet and resembles a miniature hollyhock, the flowers being of a pale golden or sulphur-yellow, 2 or 3 inches in diameter and several on a stalk.

As Tangu is approached the valley expands into broad grassy flats, and here at about 13,000 feet the vegetation rapidly diminishes in stature and abundance, and the change in species is very great. Larch, maple, cherry, and spiraea disappear, leaving willows, juniper, stunted birch, silver fir, mountain ash berberries, currant, honeysuckle, azalea, and many rhododendrons. The turfy ground is covered with gentians, potentillas, geraniums, and purple and yellow meconopsis, delphiniums, orchids, saxifrage, campanulas, ranunculus, anemones, primulas (including the magnificent *Primula Sikkimensis*), and three or four species of ferns. The country being now so much more open, the valley bottom and the mountain-sides glow with purples and yellows of various shades. Not even here, nor indeed anywhere in the Himalaya, do we see that mass and glow of colour we find in California, where wide sheets of meadow-land are ablaze with the purple of the lupins and the gold of the Californian poppy. But for the number of varieties of plants these upper valleys of the Teesta River can scarcely be excelled. As we ascend the mountain-sides above Tangu we find them covered with plants of numerous different kinds, and even at about 14,000 feet Hooker gathered over two hundred plants.

But now we are nearing the limit of plant life. At 17,000 feet the vegetation has ceased to be alpine and has become arctic, and the plants nearest the snow-line are minute primulas, saxifrages, gentians, grasses, sedges, some tufted wormwood, and a dwarf rhododendron, the most alpine of wooded plants.

At the summit of the Donkia Pass Hooker found one flowering plant, the *Arenaria rupifragia*. The fescue (*Festuca ovina*), a little fern (*Woodsia*), and a saussurea ascend very near the summit. A pink-coloured woolly saussurea and *Delphinium glaciale* are two of the most lofty plants, and are commonly found from 17,500 feet to 18,000 feet. Besides some barren mosses several lichens grow on the top, as *Cladonia vermicularis*, the yellow *Lecidea geographica* and the orange *L. miniata*.

At 18,300 feet Hooker found on one stone only a fine Scottish lichen, a species of gyrophora, the "tripe de roche" of Arctic voyagers and the food of the Canadian hunters. It is also abundant in the Scotch Alps.

On the summit of Bhomtso, 18,590 feet, the only plants were the lichens *Lecidea miniata* (or *Parmalia miniata)* mentioned above, and borrera. The first-named minute lichen is the most arctic, antarctic, alpine, and universally diffused in the world, and often occurs so abundantly as to colour the rocks an orange red.

* * *

The entire range of plant life, from the truly tropical to the hardiest arctic, is now complete. As we look back from the limit of perpetual snow we see the whole great procession in a glance. We have come across no African, nor South American, nor Australian plants, so we have not seen anything like the *whole* of plant life. But the range from the tropic to the arctic has been complete and continuous. In no other region could we in so short a space as a hundred miles—the distance from Bath to London—see the entire range so fully represented.

And actually *seeing* how vast is the range and variety of plant life is a very different thing from knowing that it exists; seeing the flowers in the flesh is altogether different from only reading descriptions of them; and seeing them in masses and in their natural surroundings affects us quite differently from seeing only a few in a garden or in a hot-house. Here on the spot we feel close in touch with Nature's own heart. We see Nature's productions springing up fresh and new straight from the very fountain source. We have the joy of being able to stretch out a hand and pick a flower direct from its own surroundings, and to fondle it, examine it all round, admire its colour, form, and texture, compare its beauty with the beauty of other flowers and settle wherein its special beauty lies. We shall never be able to give to even the most exquisite orchid or the most perfect lily the same affection that we give to the primroses and violets of our native land. But we may be sure that our Naturalist-Artist, when he gathers together in his mind the impressions which have been made upon him by his passage through the tropical forests to the alpine uplands and thence to the limit of perpetual snow, will find that his sense of the variety of beauty to be found in trees and leaves, in ferns and flowers, has immeasurably expanded. He will have acquired a firmer grasp of plant life as a whole. He will have a truer measure of the beauty in it. And irresistibly, but most willingly, he will have been more closely drawn to Nature's heart.

CHAPTER IV.
THE DENIZENS OF THE FOREST

So far we have paid attention almost exclusively to the plant life. But all through Sikkim the insect life presses itself just as insistently on our notice. In the tropical portion it is unbelievably abundant and varied. It swarms about us and is ever present. And much of it is as beautiful as the flowers. For sheer attractiveness the butterflies are as compelling as the orchids. Mosquitoes, gnats, flies, leeches, every torment there is. But we forgive everything for the chance of being able to see alive and in the full glory of their colouring these brilliant gems of the insect world which we can in places view in hundreds and thousands at a time—and in extraordinary variety, for in this little country more than six hundred species are found—about ten times as many as are met with in England. Moreover, there is no season when they are wholly absent, for in the hot valleys they may be seen all the year round, though naturally there are more in the summer than in the winter.

If it were not for other attractions we would like to concentrate our attention on these beautiful creatures alone. For they fascinate us by the daring of their colours, by their bold designs, by the way in which they blend the colours with one another, and by the extreme delicacy and chasteness of both colour and design. We are reluctant to take the life of a single one of the thousands we see, but yet we are itching, too, to lay hold of one after another as it sails into sight displaying some fresh beauty. We want to handle it as we would a flower, turn it about and examine it from every point of view till not a shade or aspect of its beauty has escaped us. In the presence of these brilliant butterflies we are children once more. We want to have them in our hands and feel that they are in our possession. It is tantalising merely to view them from a distance. We want to enjoy their beauty to the full.

These butterflies of Sikkim are such complete strangers to us we do not even know their names. From the "Gazetteer," however, we learn that the most beautiful of them are the papilios, of which alone there are no less than forty-two species. And three of these—namely, the *Teinophalus imperialis* (which occurs on Tiger Hill above Darjiling) and two ornithopteras, or bird-butterflies—are among the most splendid of all butterflies. The former is green on the upper side with yellow spots on the hind-wing, and the long tails are tipped with yellow. The two bird-butterflies are common in the low valleys from May to October. They are truly magnificent insects, measuring from 6 to 8 inches across. Their fore-wings are wholly of a velvety black and the hind-wing golden yellow scolloped with black.

Of the well-known green species of papilio, with longish tails and blue or green spots on the hindwing, there are four species, of which one is European. Some have semi-transparent wings of a lace-like pattern, with long slender tails to the hind-wings, and are of a very elegant shape.

A most gorgeously-coloured butterfly is the *Thaumantis diores*, black with large spots (which cover a great part of both fore and hind wings) of a brilliant metallic, changeable blue. It measures 4 3/4 inches across the outspread wings. It avoids the direct sunlight and dodges about among the scrub growing under the deep shade of tall trees in the hottest and moistest valleys.

One of the most lovely butterflies in the world is the *Stichophthalma camadeva*, which is one of the largest of the Sikkim butterflies, being from 5 to 6 1/2 inches in expanse. It is more soberly coloured on the upper side than the last-named, being chiefly white and brown, but the underside is more beautiful, having a row of five red ocelli with black irides on each wing and other pretty markings.

The lyccenides, or "blues," are represented by no less than 154 species, several of them of surpassing beauty. Many are marked with changeable metallic hues on the upper side of the fore-wing: some violet, some with green, and some with golden bronze. The most lovely of all is the *Ilerea brahma*, of which the colouring of the upper side of the male is unique.

Then there is the curious leaf-butterfly, which has a marvellous resemblance to a dead leaf with its wings folded over the back and showing the underside only, the leaf-stalk veins being excellently mimicked. But when flying about its upper side, which is a deep violet-blue with a conspicuous yellowish bar across the fore-wing, is exposed, and the butterfly is then most beautiful. I have seen many of these lovely butterflies flying about in the Teesta Valley, glistening in the dappled light of the forest, and then settle on a branch; and unless I had actually seen them alight, I should never have known them from leaves.

* * *

The moths, though naturally not as beautiful as the butterflies, are far more numerous, there being something like two thousand species. Several of them are the largest of the insect race. And one of them, the famous atlas moth, is sometimes nearly a foot across. Next in size come several species of the genus *Actias*, of which *selene* is the most common. It is of a pale green colour with a pinkish; spot, and has long slender tails. It measures about 8 inches across the fore-wings, and nearly as much from shoulder to the tip of the tail.

* * *

Other insects numerously represented in Sikkim are beetles, bugs, grasshoppers, praying insects, walking-stick insects, dragon-flies, ants, lantern-flies, cicadae, etc.

* * *

Plant life and insect life are abundant enough, but of birds there seem to be comparatively few. As we travel through the forest we do not notice many of them, and we do not hear many. We do not everywhere find great flocks of birds as we see swarms of insects. And we do not find the forest resounding with the songs of birds as it does with the hum and crackle of insects. In this respect we are disappointed.

But the birds of Sikkim, if few in number, are great in variety. Birds feed on fruits, berries, seeds, insects, grubs, caterpillars, small animals, and even little birds. Some birds like a still, hot, damp climate. Other birds like a cold, dry climate. Some birds like the shade and quiet and protection of the forest. Others like the open and the sunshine. Some birds find their food in the water, others on the land. And the Sikkim Himalaya, from the plains to the mountains, provides such a rich variety of plant and insect life, such a variety of climate and of country, and so plentiful a supply of water, that birds of the widest difference of requirements can here be provided with their needs.

Consequently birds of numerous different species make Sikkim their habitat, either permanently or for certain seasons of the year. And Gammie, who has specially studied the natural history of Sikkim, says in the "Sikkim Gazetteer" that in no part of the world of an equal area are birds more profusely represented in species. The birds may not be so numerous as in other parts, but they are more varied. Between five and six hundred species are represented, varying from the great vulture known as the lammergeyer, which is 9 1/2 feet across the outstretched wing, down to the tiny flower-pecker, barely exceeding 3 inches from the end of its beak to the tip of its tail.

Of the birds found in the forest itself, the honey-suckers or sun-birds are perhaps the most beautiful. There are no gorgeous birds of paradise, and even resplendent parrots are not very numerous. But these little sun-birds glitter like jewels among the leafy foliage, and the lustrous metallic hues of different shades with which they are richly coloured on the head and long tail-feathers change and flash in the sunlight with every slightest movement.

The Heart Of Nature Or The Quest For Natural Beauty | 37

Not all so brilliant in colour but very delightful to watch are the fly-catchers. Of these there are no less than twenty-six species, the most remarkable being the fairy blue-chat, which is brilliantly marked with different shades of glistening blue, and another which is strikingly coloured in almost uniform verditer blue. In the very lowest valleys is found the beautiful paradise fly-catcher, with a long-pointed black crest, the rest of the plumage white with black shafts and the tail 14 inches in length. The quickness and agility this lovely bird displays as it darts and twists and turns in the pursuit of butterflies in their uneven dodging flight is one of the marvels of forest life.

Game-birds are not abundant, but four species of pheasant are found, of which the largest and handsomest is the moonal, bronze-green glossed with gold and with a tail of cinnamon red. Sportsmen in the Himalaya are familiar with the sight of this radiantly-coloured bird swishing down the mountain-side with apparently the speed and almost the brilliancy of a flash of lightning. Not so handsome as the moonal, being small and greyish in colour on the back, is the blood-pheasant, remarkable for its blood-red streaks on the breast and its blood-red under-tail-coverts.

Bulbuls are largely represented and may be seen in large flocks among the scrub—delightful, homely little birds with bright and cheery ways which specially attract us. Not very common, but to be found in the lower part of the valley, is the beautiful fairy bluebird, a large bird 10 inches in length with a glistening cobalt-blue upper part and velvet black beneath. The European cuckoo may be heard all day long in the season from about 3,500 feet upwards. And about a dozen other cuckoos visit Sikkim, of which by far the prettiest is the emerald cuckoo, a small bird not much more than 6 inches long, of a brilliant emerald green with golden sheen, and below white barred with shining green. Kingfishers are not numerous, as fish are scarce. But there are four species, of which the prettiest is a lovely little creature about 5 inches long, coloured with rufous, white, and different shades of blue and violet.

These are only a few of the most striking birds; but to give an idea of the variety of other birds which may be found in Sikkim, many of which are hardly less beautiful than those above described, we may learn from Gammie that among the birds of prey there are eleven eagles; the peregrine falcon, a little pigmy falcon, and five other falcons; a big brown wood-owl, 2 feet in length, a pigmy owlet measuring only 6 inches, and nine other owls; and six kites;— among the game-birds, besides pheasants, three quails, two hill-partridges, a jungle-fowl, woodcock, a snow-cock, and a snow-partridge;—among other classes of birds, nine or ten species of pigeons and doves; the European raven and a jungle crow; one jay and several magpies; two hornbills, one of which is 4 feet in length; the common and the Nepal swallow; about thirty species of finches, among them being three bullfinches and eight rose-finches; three or four larks; numerous and varied tits; wagtails; five species of parrots; eight or nine species of wren; thrushes of a dozen species; ten species of robin; and, lastly, many species of waders such as florekin, cranes, plovers, snipe, sandpipers, coots, water-hen, storks, heron, cormorants, terns, divers, and ducks.

* * *

Reptiles are not commonly accounted among the beauties of Nature; but they must not be lost sight of in reviewing the life of the forest. The largest is the python, whose usual length is 12 feet, though individuals of 16 to 20 feet are not very rare. A very beautiful snake found in the cool forests is green with a broad black band on each side of the hinder half of the body and tail, the green scales being margined with black. Another snake of the same length is a handsome green whip-snake, graceful in its movements, but ferocious and aggressive in its habits, although quite harmless. The ordinary cobra is not uncommon. The giant cobra is also found in the lower valleys, and grows to a length of 12 or 13 feet. Four species of pit vipers are found. The krait occurs, but is not common. Altogether there are nine species of venomous snakes and thirty species of non-venomous snakes found in Sikkim.

Of lizards there are ten species. One is popularly known as the chameleon on account of its rather showy colours, but does not really belong to that family. And a beautiful grass-snake, which, as it is limbless, is often mistaken for a tree-snake, is also of the lizard genus.

Of frogs and toads there are about sixteen species. Among them are several prettily-coloured tree-frogs. Several of the species are recognised by their call.

* * *

Of mammals about eighty-one species are found. They include three monkeys, eight of the cat tribe, two civet cats, one tree cat, two mongooses, two of the dog tribe, five pole-cats and weasels, one ferret-badger, three otters, one cat-bear, two bears, one tree-shrew, one mole, six shrews, two water-shrews, twelve bats, four squirrels, two marmots, eight rats and mice, one vole, one porcupine, four deer, two forest-goats, one goat, one sheep, and one ant-eater.

The common monkey of India, the Bengal monkey, is found in large companies at low elevations. The Himalayan monkey is abundant from 3,000 to 6,000 feet; and the Himalayan langur frequents the zone from 7,000 to 12,000 feet.

The tiger inhabits the Terai at the foot of the mountains, but is only an occasional visitor to Sikkim proper. But the leopard and the clouded leopard are permanent residents and fairly common. This last is of a most beautiful mottled colouring. Another leopard is the snow-leopard, which inhabits high altitudes only. The marbled-cat is a miniature edition of the clouded leopard, and the leopard-cat of the common leopard. The large Indian civet-cat is not uncommon, but the spotted tiger-civet, a very beautiful and active creature, is rare. The jackal is not uncommon, and there is at least one species of wild-dog. These dogs hunt in packs and kill wild-pig, deer, goats, etc. A very peculiar and interesting animal is the cat-bear, which has the head and arms of a minute bear and the tail of a cat. The brown bear occurs at high altitudes, and the Himalayan black bear is common lower down. The black hill squirrel is a large handsome animal of the lower forests, and a very handsome flying squirrel inhabits the forests between 5,000 and 10,000 feet.

The great Sikkim stag is not found in Sikkim proper, but inhabits the Chumbi Valley. The sambhar stag is abundant. The commonest of the deer tribe is the khakar, or barking deer. It is, says Hodgson, unmatched for flexibility and power of creeping through tangled underwood. The musk deer remains at high elevations.

In addition to the above, elephants come up from the forests in the plains, and in these plain forests are found (besides tigers and boars) rhinoceros, bison, and buffalo.

* * *

This has been a long enumeration of the animal life, in its many branches, which is found in the forest. The mere cataloguing of it is sufficient to show the extent and variety of insect, bird, reptile, and mammal life which the forest contains. But it is with the beauty of this animal life, rather than with its extent and variety, that we are concerned. And if the Artist is to see its full beauty, he must see it with the eyes of the naturalist and sportsman—men whose eyes are trained to observe in minutest detail the form and colour and character of each animal, bird, or insect, and who know something of the life each has to lead, and the conditions in which it is placed. More sportsmen than naturalists, and more naturalists than artists, observe these and other animals in their natural surroundings. But, nowadays, at least photographers and cinematographers are going into the wilds to portray them. And perhaps naturalist-artists will arise who, every bit as keen as sportsmen now are to get to close quarters with game animals, will want to get into positions from which they will be able carefully to observe animals of all kinds and take note of every characteristic. These artists will have to be fully as alert as the sportsmen, and be able on the instant, and from a fleeting glimpse, to note the lines and shades and character of the animal. But, if they do this, they will, in all probability, bring back more lasting and deeper impressions of the animals than the sportsman with all his keen observation ever receives — and they will enjoy a greater pleasure. An artist, who from observing an animal in its own haunts, and from the sketches and notes he made there, could paint a picture of it in its own surroundings, would assuredly derive more pleasure from his enterprise than the sportsman who simply brought back the animal's head. In addition he would have enabled others to share his enjoyment with him. There is a great field here for the painter; and many would welcome a change from the same old cows and sheep tamely grazing in a meadow, which is all that artists usually present to us of animal life.

Among the most conspicuous animals met with are the elephant, the bison, the buffalo, and the rhinoceros. And it would be hard to discover beauty in any of these. As we see the rhinoceros, for example, in the Zoological Gardens nothing could be more ugly. Yet we should not despair of finding beauty even in a rhinoceros if we could study him in his natural surroundings and understand all the circumstances of his life. If we observed him and his habits and habitat with the knowledge of the naturalist and the keenness of the sportsman, we might find that in his form and colour he does in his own peculiar fashion fitly express the purpose of his being. And whatever adequately expresses a definite purpose is beautiful. Where a dainty antelope would be altogether out of place, the ponderous rhinoceros may be completely in his element. Where a tender-skinned horse would be driven mad by insects, the thick-skinned beast passes the time untroubled. In a drawing-room a daintily-dressed lady is a vision of loveliness. In a ploughed field she would look ridiculous. In a drawing-room a peasant would look uncouth. In a field, as Millet has shown us, he possesses a beauty, dignified and touching. It is not impossible, therefore, that an artist who had the opportunity of entering into the life of a rhinoceros, as Millet had of entering into the life of a peasant, might discover beauty even in that monstrosity. This, however, I allow is an extreme case.

In a less extreme case beauty has already been discovered. The bison does not at first sight strike us as a beautiful animal. Yet Mr. Stebbing, the naturalist-sportsman, says that, as he caught sight of one after a long stalk, and watched it with palpitating heart, he was fascinated by the grand sight — 18 hands of coal-black beauty shining like satin in the light filtering through the branches of the trees.

When we move on from the bison to the stag the beauty is evident enough. A stag carries himself right royally, and has a rugged, majestic beauty all his own. There are few more beautiful sights in the animal world than that of a lordly stag standing tense with preparedness to turn swiftly, and, on the instant, bound away in any direction.

Not majestic like the great deer, but of a more airy grace and daintiness, are the smaller deer and antelope. The lightness of their tread, their suppleness of movement, and their spring and litheness, fill us with delight.

* * *

We now come to the crown of the animal kingdom—man. And in the Sikkim Himalaya are to be found men of all the stages of civilisation from the most primitive to the most advanced. Inhabiting the forests at the foot of the mountains are certain jungle peoples of extreme interest simply by reason of their primitiveness. They represent the very early stages of man, and in observing them in their own haunts, we shall understand something of the immensity and the delicacy of man's task in gaining his ascendancy in the animal world and acquiring a greater mastery over his surroundings.

In these forests teeming with animal life of all kinds man had to hold his own against dangerous and stronger animals, and to supply himself with food in the face of many rivals. He had to be as alert as the sharpest-witted and as cunning as the most crafty, and to have physical fitness and endurance to stand the strain of incessant rivalry. This is what these jungle people have. Their alertness, their capacity to glide through the forest almost as stealthily as an animal, their keenness of sight, their acute sense of hearing, their knowledge of jungle lore and of the habits of animals, and their ability to stand long and hard physical strain, are the envy of us civilised men when we find ourselves among them. Particularly is this shown when tracking. They will note the slightest indication of the passage of the animal they are after—the faintest footprint, a stone overturned and showing the moisture on its under surface, a broken twig, a bitten leaf, the bark rubbed—and they will be able to judge from the exact appearance of these signs how long it is since the animal made them. They will, too, detect sounds which we civilised men would certainly never hear, and from a note of alarm in these sounds, or from excitement among birds, infer the presence of a dangerous animal.

When seen outside the forests these jungle men look wild and unkempt, but seen in their natural surroundings and compared *there* with the white man, they have a Beauty which is wanting in the white man. In *these* surroundings they have a dignity and composure and assurance which the European lacks. They are on their own ground, and there they are beautiful.

And these primitive men are worthy of being painted by the very greatest of painters, and of having their praises sung by the very first of poets. For it is they and their like who, with only such weapons as the forest affords and

42 | The Heart Of Nature Or The Quest For Natural Beauty

their own ingenuity devised, won the way through for us civilised men, won the battle against the fierce and much more powerful beasts around them, and by great daring and through sheer skill, courage, and endurance led the way to the light. It was a marvellous feat. For all the privileges and immunities which we men of to-day enjoy we have to thank these primitive forest men, and our gratitude could never be too great. They are deserving of the closest attention and the warmest appreciation.

Not many of these really primitive peoples are nowadays left in the jungles. But the tea-gardens have attracted a primitive people, the Santals, who are typical of the true Dravidian stock of India—a jolly, cheerful, easy-going, and, on the whole, law-abiding, truthful, and honest people who love a roaming life, with plenty of hunting and fishing.

The Lepchas of Sikkim have risen above the first primitive stage. They clothe themselves well and dwell in well-built houses. They do not possess for us the same essential interest as belongs to truly primitive people. But on account of their intimate knowledge of the forest and its denizens, and by reason also of their being a remarkably simple, gentle, and likeable people, they have an unusual attraction for travellers. Hooker, who was one of the first to live among them, and Claude White, who lived among them for many years, both write of them in affectionate terms. They are child-like and engaging, good-humoured, cheery and amiable, free and unrestrained. They have, too, a reputation for honesty and truthfulness.

More vigorous, capable, and virile than the Lepchas are the Nepalese, who, migrating from Nepal, are found in great numbers in this region. They are more given to agriculture than the Lepchas, and are thrifty, industrious, and resourceful. Though excitable and aggressive, they are also law-abiding.

Less numerous but prominent inhabitants of this region are the Bhutias, who consist of four classes; Bhutias, who are a mixed race of Tibetans and Lepchas; Sherpa Bhutias, who come from the east of Nepal, the word *sher* merely meaning "east"; the Drukpa or Dharma Bhutias, whose home is Bhutan; and the Tibetan Bhutias from Tibet. They are strong, sturdy men, merry and cheerful.

These Lepchas, Nepalese, and Bhutias are all of Mongolian origin, and therefore have the distinctively Mongolian appearance. But besides these, in Darjiling and on the tea-gardens are to be found Bengali clerks, Marwari merchants from Rajputana, Punjabi traders, Hindustani mechanics, and Chinese carpenters. And in addition to all these are British Government officials, tea-planters, and a continual stream of visitors from all parts of Europe and America, who come to Darjiling to view the snowy range.

So that in this small region may be found representatives of every grade of civilisation and a great variety of types. And what an amount of Beauty— as distinct from mere prettiness—there is to discover in even the rough local people may be seen from the pictures of the Russian painter Verestchagin, engravings from which are given in his autobiographical sketches entitled "Vassili Verestchagin." This great painter evidently succeeded in getting inside the wild peoples he loved; and his pictures reveal to us beauties we might without them never have known. In these people's gait, their attitudes, their grouping, as well as in their features, he was able to discern the hardihood, the patience, the impetuosity, the gentleness of their character, and portray it for us.

Putting aside the obvious differences between us and them, we are able to detect our fundamental identity of nature, have a fellow-feeling with them, recognise sameness between us and so see their beauty.

CHAPTER V.
THE SUM IMPRESSION

The Artist has now to stand back and view the forest as a whole. And he must test his view in the light of reason—bring Truth to bear upon Beauty. The forest with its multitudinous and varied life, ranging from simplest to most cultured man, is an epitome of Nature so far as she is manifested on this planet. And he will from this epitome try to get a view of the real character of Nature. As he takes stock of the impressions which have been made upon him, he will have to form a conclusion of absolutely fundamental importance for the enjoyment of Natural Beauty.

Men's hearts instinctively go out to Nature, and in consequence they see Beauty in her. As children they love flowers and love animals. And the most primitive races have the same feeling though they are just as callous in their treatment of animals as children are in their treatment of one another. In the more cultured races this instinctive love of Nature and appreciation of Natural Beauty has enormously developed. But if men ever came to hold the idea—as so many since the doctrine of the survival of the fittest has come into prominence are inclined to do—that Nature is at heart cold and hard, and recks nothing of human joys and sorrows, then love of Nature would fade away from men's hearts. Being out of sympathy and repelled from entering into deep communion with her, men would never again see Beauty in her. The enjoyment of Natural Beauty would pass from them for ever.

So the Artist will try to get at the true Heart of Nature. If the Naturalist part of him tells him that at bottom Nature is merciless and unrelenting, utterly regardless of the things of most worth in life; that Nature is indeed "red in tooth and claw"; that all she cares for—all she selects as the fittest to survive—are the merely strongest, the most pushing and aggressive, the individuals who will simply trample down their neighbours in order that they themselves may "survive"; or if, again, the Naturalist convinces him that all he has seen in the forest has come about by pure chance; that it is by a mere fluke that we find orchids and not mushrooms, men and not monkeys, at the head of plant and animal life; and that Nature herself is wholly indifferent as to which of the two establishes its preeminence—then he will feel the chill upon his soul, he will shrivel up within himself, the very fountain-spring of Beauty will be frozen up, and never again will he see Beauty in any single one of Nature's manifestations.

But if, on the other hand, the Naturalist is able to convince the Artist that in spite of the very evident struggle for existence Nature does not care twopence whether the "fittest" survive or not so long as what is best in the end prevails; that far from things coming about by mere chance Nature has a distinct end in view, and that end the accomplishment of what he himself most prizes, then the heart of the Artist will warm to the heart of Nature with a fervour it had never known before; his heart will throb with her heart, and every beauty he has seen in plain or mountain, in flower, bird, or man, will be a hundredfold increased.

Which of these two views of Nature, so far as Nature can be judged from what we see of her on this planet, is correct, he has now to determine. The profound mystery which everywhere prevails in the forest and which exerts such a compelling spell upon us he will want to probe to the bottom. He will not be content with the outward prettiness of butterfly and orchid, or with the mere profusion and variety of life, or with the colossal size of animals and trees. He will want to burrow down and get at the very root and mainspring of this forest life. He will want to reach the very Heart of Nature here manifested in such manifold variety. He will want to arrive at the inner significance of all this variety of life. Then only will he understand Nature and be able to decide whether Nature is cruel and therefore to be feared, or kind and gracious and therefore to be loved.

* * *

Now, when we go into the forest and look into it in detail, the profusion is even greater than we expected. In this damp tropical region where there is ample heat and moisture, plant life comes springing out of the earth with a prolificness which seems inexhaustible. And when plant life is abundant, animal and insect life is abundant also. So profuse, indeed, is the output of living things that it seems simply wasteful. A single tree may produce thousands of flowers. Each flower may have dozens of seeds. The tree may go on flowering for a hundred or two hundred years. So a single tree may produce millions of seeds, each capable of growing into a forest giant like its parent.

With insect life the same profusion of life is evident. A single moth or butterfly lays thousands of eggs. Mosquitoes, flies, gnats, midges, leeches swarm in myriads upon myriads.

The abundance and superabundance of life is the first outstanding—though it will prove not the most important—impression made upon us by a contemplation of the forest as a whole.

* * *

Scarcely less striking than the abundance is the variety. Life does not spring up from the earth in forms as alike one another as two peas. Each individual plant or animal, however small, however simple, has its own distinctive characteristics, There is variety and variation everywhere. Variety in form, variety in colour, variety in size, variety in character and habit. In size there is the difference between the huge *terminalia* towering up 200 feet high and the tiny little potentilla; between the atlas moth 12 inches in spread and the hardly discernible midges; between the elephant, massive enough to trample its way through the densest forest, and the humble little mouse peeping out of its hole in the ground. In colour the difference ranges from the light blue of the forget-me-not to the deep blue of the gentian; from the delicate pink of the dianthus to the deep crimson of the rhododendron; from the brilliant hues of the orchids to the dull browns and greens of inconspicuous tree flowers; from the vivid light greens, yellows, and reds of the young leaves of these tropical forests to the greyer green of their maturity; from the smiting reds and blues of the most gaudy butterflies, beetles, and dragon-flies to the modest browns of night-flying moths; from the gorgeous colours of the parrots to the familiar black of crows; from the yellow-striped tiger to the earth-coloured hare; from the dark-skinned aborigine to the yellow-skinned Mongolian and the fair European. Similarly do plants and animals vary in form: from the straight pines and palms to the spreading, umbrageous oaks and laurels; from upstanding lilies to parasitical orchids; from monstrous spiky beetles to symmetrical dragon-flies; from ungainly rhinoceros to graceful antelope; from short, sturdy Bhutias to tall, slim Hindustanis. Likewise in character individuals are as different as the strong, firm tree standing open-faced, four-square to all the world and the creeping, insinuating parasite; as the intelligent, industrious ant and the clumsy, plodding beetle; as the plucky boar and the timid hare; as the rough forest tribesman and the cultured Bengali.

Lastly, there is variety among not only the different species of plants, animals, insects, etc., but also the individuals of the same species. We ourselves know the differences there are between one man and another, and as far as that goes between ourselves on one day and ourselves on the next. Each plant—and still more each animal—has its own unique individuality. Every cavalry officer, every shepherd, every dog-owner, every pigeon-fancier knows that each horse, sheep, dog, pigeon has its own individuality and is distinctly different from all others of its kind. And so does every gardener

The Heart Of Nature Or The Quest For Natural Beauty | 47

know that each rose, each tulip, each pansy is different from all other roses, tulips, and pansies. It is the same in the forest. Hardly two trees or plants of the same species develop their young leaves, open their flowers, ripen their seeds, and drop their leaves at the same time. Apart from the size of the flower and leaf there are differences in colour, shape, and marking. Each in appearance and in habit has an individuality of its own.

Such is the variety in the abundant life of the forest that no two individuals, no two blades of grass, or no two leaves are in every detail precisely alike. And this is the second outstanding impression we receive.

* * *

The abundance and variety of life are evident enough. Not so evident but equally noteworthy is the intensity. In the still forest one of the giant trees looks utterly impassive and immobile. It stands there calm and unmoved. Not a leaf stirs. Yet the whole and every minutest part of it is instinct with intensest life. It is made up of countless microscopic cells in unceasing activity. Highly sensitive and mobile cells form the root-tips and insinuate their way into every crevice in search of food for the tree, rejecting what is unpalatable and forwarding what is useful for building up and sustaining the monarch. Other cells take in necessary food from the air. Others build up the trunk and its protective bark. Others, and most important of all, go to make up the flowers of the tree and the organs of reproduction which enable the tree to propagate its kind.

All this activity of the separate cells and combinations of cells is taking place. And in addition there is that activity of them all in their togetherness, that activity which keeps the cells together, and which if relaxed for a moment would mean that the cells would all collapse as the grains of dust in an eddying dust-devil at a street corner collapse once the gust of wind which stirred them and keeps them together drops away. What must be the intensity of life required to develop the tree from the seed and to rear that giant straight up from the level soil 200 feet into the air and maintain it there two hundred years, we can only imagine; for to outward appearance the tree is quite impassive. It does not move a muscle of its face to reveal the intensity of life within.

The tree is characteristic of every living thing. Every plant and every animal, however seemingly sluggish, is working to fulfil its life, to nourish itself, to reproduce its kind.

* * *

Now, the amount of air and sunshine for plants may be practically unlimited, but air and sunshine are not all that plants require. They want soil and moisture as well. And the standing-room for plants is strictly limited. The forest stretches away up to the snows; but there it stops. Necessarily, therefore, there must be the keenest and most incessant struggle among the plants for standing-room. Only a comparatively few can be accommodated. The rest cannot survive. And as the number of plants which can survive is thus limited, the number of animals is limited also, for animals are dependent on plants. Plants, therefore, in spite of their eminently pacific appearance are engaged in a fierce struggle with one another for standing-room. And animals are likewise engaged in a struggle among themselves for the plants.

There is competition among the roots of the different individual plants for the food and water of the soil. And there is competition among the leaves for the sunlight. Each plant is pushing its roots downwards and spreading outward for more food and to root itself more firmly. Each is straining upward to receive more sunlight. Each is struggling with its fellows for room and means to develop its life. Competitors in hundreds and thousands are forced to withdraw and succumb. And even when a forest giant has defeated all competitors and reached its full maturity it has still to maintain the struggle and hold its own continually against other individuals whose roots are reaching out below and whose branches are spreading out above; against climbers who would smother it; and against parasites who would suck its very life-blood. The battle, moreover, is often not so much between one species and another species as between individuals of the same species. And it is a war which continues through life.

The struggle for existence among the plants and trees is keen beyond imagination. And the struggle among the insects, birds and beasts, and man for the plants and products of the trees is no less severe. So now our impression is that of an abundant, varied and intense life in which the individuals are perpetually struggling with one another for bare existence.

* * *

Under these stringent and stressful conditions does each living being come into the world. He has to battle his way through—or succumb. Plants as well as men, and men as well as plants. So, as we look into the structure of animals and plants, we are not surprised to find that in order to cope with their surroundings they have developed organs which are specially adapted to enable them to secure the needful food, to hold their own against the competition of their neighbours, to meet the exigencies of their surroundings, and to pursue their own life to the full extent of its possibilities. Even plants are like sentient beings in this respect. The sensitive tips of their roots are organs admirably adapted for feeling their way through the soil and selecting from its constituents what will best nourish the plant. The leaves opening out to the air and sunshine are other organs adapted for gathering in nourishment. And thorns and poisonous juices are means adapted to fend off destructive neighbours. The eyes and ears in animals are other instances of organs which enable them to see what will serve them as food, or to hear what may be possible enemies, and to make use of what will help them to the proper fulfilment of their life.

We see each individual plant and animal striving to the best of his ability to adjust himself to the conditions in which he finds himself, trying to adapt himself to his surroundings—to his physical surroundings, such as the climate and soil, and to his social surroundings, consisting of his plant and animal neighbours and rivals. We shall probably notice, too, that he seems to be driven by some inner impulse (which in its turn is a responding to the impress of the totality of the individual's surroundings) to strive to do something more than merely adapt himself to his surroundings. He is urged on to rise superior to them.

So the course of the individual's life is continually being affected by surroundings which compel him to adapt himself to them on pain of extinction if he fails. On the other hand, he is himself, in his own small way, affecting his surroundings and causing *them* to adapt themselves to *him*. Even the humblest plant takes from the surrounding soil and air what it needs as food and changes it in the process of assimilation, so that the surroundings are, to a slight extent at least, changed by the activity of the plant. And we already have noticed how a plant's insect surroundings have to adapt themselves to the plant. There is reciprocal action, therefore—the surroundings forcing the individual to adapt himself to them, and the individual causing the surroundings to adapt themselves to him.

Here we have reached the point where, besides the struggle for existence among the individuals of an abundant, varied, and intense life, there is adaptation among the individuals to their surroundings and of their surroundings to the individuals.

* * *

We have now to note how with the adaptation goes selection. Set amid these physical and organic surroundings, some helpful, some harmful, the individual has to spend his life in selecting and rejecting what will further or hinder his natural development. He has to reject much, for there is much that will harm him. He has to select a little—for that little is vitally necessary for his upbuilding and maintenance. From among the elements of the soil he has to choose those particular elements that he needs. Thus a plant selects through its roots from the elements of the soil, and through its leaves from the elements of the air, those elements and in those quantities that it needs for nourishment and growth. But it has also, by means of thorns or poison juices or other device, to protect itself from being itself selected by some animal for that animal's own nourishment and growth.

So the individual is constantly selecting, and is as constantly on the guard against being selected. The principle of selection among the abundant and varied life is in continual operation. And unless he selects wisely he will not survive; for he will either have insufficient to live on or else have what is harmful to his life. Nor will he survive unless he is able to fend off those who would select him for their own maintenance. There is selection everywhere—selection *by* the individual and selection *of* the individual by surrounding neighbours and circumstances.

* * *

Thus far we have only recapitulated what most men are familiar with since Darwin commenced preaching the doctrine of Evolution by Natural Selection sixty years ago. But the Naturalist-Artist of the future will probably not be content with the conclusion to which so many jump that all that Nature teaches or expects of individuals—plants, beasts, or men—is that they should adapt themselves to their surroundings and fit themselves to survive; that all Nature has at heart is adaptability of individuals to their surroundings and their fitness to survive. The lowly amoeba can perform these unenterprising functions more fitly than himself. And the Artist would never be satisfied with so mean and meagre an ambition as merely to adapt himself to his surroundings and fit himself to survive. If he saw evidence of no higher expectation than that in the workings of Nature, his heart would certainly not cleave to her heart. And there being estrangement and coolness between his heart and hers, he would see no Beauty in Nature and his pursuit of Natural Beauty might here end.

But an instinct within him tells him that this cannot be the last word as to Nature's character and methods. He himself is constantly risking his life with no thought of trying to survive, and he sees his neighbours doing the same. And his inclination is to go a good deal farther than tamely adapting himself to his surroundings. He wants and strives to rise superior to them—and he finds his neighbours likewise striving. So with this instinct goading him on he is driven to probe deeper still into the mystery of the forest life.

* * *

Of selection and adaptation we have seen evidence throughout the whole forest life. Now, where there is selection and where there is adaptation there must be *purposiveness*. Selection implies the power of choice, and we have seen how plants as well as animals deliberately and effectively exercise this power of choice. And adaptation implies adjustment to an end, and we have seen how wonderfully plants no less than animals adapt themselves to certain ends. And where individuals have the power of choice and exercise that power; and where they have the power of adapting themselves to certain ends and exercise that power, there obviously is purposiveness.

Purposiveness runs like a streak through every activity. It permeates the whole forest life. It is observable in plants no less than in animals. Naturalists, indeed, regard trees and plants as truly sentient beings. And the means plants employ to compass the end they have in view, are truly wonderful. Still more remarkable is the fact that hardly two attain their object by exactly the same means. The tropical forest is full of climbing plants bent upon reaching the sunlight. But some climb by coiling round the trunk of a tree like a snake, some swarm up it by holding on with claws, some ascend by means of adhering aerial roots, and some reach what they want by pushing through a tangle of branches spreading out arms and hauling themselves up. And when plants have attained maturity and flowered, the flowers employ numberless ways of attracting insects for the purpose of fertilisation. In a still, tropical forest, such as that of Lower Sikkim, there is no hope of the pollen being carried from one flower to another by air-currents. The flowers have therefore to devise a means for the transport of the pollen. Efforts are made to induce winged creatures—insects in most cases, but sometimes birds—to render assistance. Colours for day-flying insects and scent for night-flying insects are accordingly employed as means to this end. Brilliant colours attract butterflies and bees by day. Strong scent—sometimes pleasant to our taste, sometimes the reverse—attracts moths and other insects by night. And the flowers which depend on their scents and not on colour are usually white or dull brown or green. And this scent is not exhaled when it is not needed, but only when the insects which the flowers wish to attract are about.

Orchids especially seem to *know* what they want. Their aerial roots wander about in search of what they want and seem to smell their way. They use discrimination in utilising their knowledge. They *choose*. And each individual seems to choose in its own way. From among many means of achieving the same end they make a definite choice, and different plants make different choices—they use different means.

Plants, therefore, quite evidently employ means to an end. They have an end in view—sometimes their own maintenance, sometimes the perpetuation of their kind, sometimes something else—and they employ means to achieve that end. They are, that is to say, *purposive* in their nature.

* * *

Evidence of purposiveness is also furnished by the wonderful organs of adaptation, root-tips, leaves, eyes, lungs, etc. It is extremely improbable that they came into being—or even started to come into being—by mere chance alone. The odds are countless millions to one against the atoms, molecules, and cells—myriads in number—of any one of these organs of adaptation having by mere chance grouped themselves in such a way as to form an effective eye, or lung, or leaf. It is, literally speaking, infinitely improbable that the organs of adaptation we see in a forest, in plant and animal, should have come into existence through chance alone.

The organs of adaptation are distinctly and definitely purposive structures—not purposed, perhaps, but certainly purposeful. In its struggle with its surroundings and with competitors the individual has been compelled to bring into being organs to fulfil a purpose. It is not the case that the organ was first created and then a use found for it, or use made of it. What actually happens is that first there is a vague but insistent reaching out towards an end, towards the fulfilment of some inner want or need—the need for food or to propagate, or whatever it may be—and that to achieve that end, or fulfil that need, the individual is driven to create a special organisation—as an Air Ministry was created during the War to fulfil the new need for fighting in the air—and so a new organ is produced: an essentially purposive structure such as the eye or the lung, though unpurposed before the need arose. The organs we see, therefore, are outward and visible signs of the existence within of a definite striving towards an end—that is, of a purpose.

The forest shows an abundant, varied, and intense life in which individuals are for ever battling with one another. But all is not happening by chance. Everywhere we see signs of purposiveness. Purposiveness—the striving towards an end—stands out as a dominating feature in forest life. Selections and adaptations are made, but they are made with some purpose in view. Purpose governs the adaptations and selections. What that purpose is we shall try and discover as we get to know still more of Nature.

* * *

So far we have been observing individuals as separate individuals. Now we must look at them gathered together as a whole. And the first point we note is that though each individual has his own unique individuality, whether he be plant or man, all are kept together as a single whole. We have seen the individuals battling with one another, competing with one another, struggling against one another. But that is only one side of the picture. Just as remarkable as the way in which they have to resist one another is the way in which they depend on one another. Their interdependence is, therefore, the point we have now to note.

Since Darwin drew our attention to the struggle for existence and survival of the fittest, the perpetual strife in Nature has been clear enough. But hard, selfish, cruel, brutal though the struggle frequently is, though the strong will often trample mercilessly on the weak and let the unfit go to the wall without any consideration whatever; yet the very strongest and fittest individual could not survive for a moment by itself alone. And what is just as remarkable as the struggle between individuals is their dependence upon one another.

All plants depend upon the natural elements—the soil, water, air, and light. Animals depend on plants. And many animals depend upon other animals. A forest tree in its maturity is covered with blossoms, some conspicuous, others inconspicuous to sight, but very conspicuous to smell. These blossoms, either by sight or scent, attract butterflies, bees, moths, and other insects to sip their nectar, and in so doing carry away the pollen of the flowers, and unwittingly pass it on to another flower and fertilise it. The insect thus enables the tree to procreate its species. But the butterfly, after sipping the nectar of the flower of the tree, deposits its eggs on the under surface of the leaves, and the leaves give nourishment to the caterpillars into which these eggs develop. Besides this, the flowers, having been fertilised by the insects, develop into fruits or berries containing seeds; and these fruits, berries, and seeds form food for monkeys, birds, bats, and rodents. In quarrelling for these many are dropped and form food for mice and others below. Birds, finding food so near, pair, build their nests, and bring up their young in its branches. And in addition to the birds which are attracted by the berries, fruits, and seeds, other birds which are attracted by the caterpillars come there and build their nests. Without the flowers the bees would be starved; without the bees or other insects the flowers would not be fertilised and the tree would not perpetuate itself.[*]

[*] I take this illustration from Rodway's "In the Guiana Forest." It applies equally to any tropical forest.

The lives of all individuals, whether plants, beasts, or men, are thus curiously interwoven with and interdependent on one another. They are also dependent upon the chemical elements in the soil and air. And even then the dependence does not cease, for they depend, too, upon the light and heat from the Sun. And the Sun itself, and this Earth as well, are subtly connected with the whole Stellar Universe.

It is only within limits that any individual can be regarded as a distinct and separate entity. It has its own unique individuality, it is true. But it is also connected with all the rest of the forest and with all the rest of the Earth, of the Solar System, and of the Universe. Each individual is to *some* extent dependent upon all other individuals. All influence and are influenced by all the rest.

There is mutual influence everywhere. And all are connected in a whole—the whole influencing each individual and each individual influencing the whole.

So besides the resistance of individuals to one another, there is attraction. Besides conflict there is co-operation. Besides independence there is interdependence.

The life of the forest thus forms a whole. Individuals have their due allowance of freedom. But they are kept together in a whole. Running through the individuals in their ensemble, binding them together, in spite of the tether they are allowed, must therefore be some kind of Organising Activity. We cannot look into that marvellous forest life without seeing that at the back of it, working all the way through it, controlling, guiding, inspiring every movement, is some dominating Activity, which, while allowing individuals freedom for experimenting by the process of trial and error, yet keeps them all bound together as a whole. And when we note the evidence of purposiveness everywhere so abundant, we cannot resist the conclusion that this Activity also gives *direction*.

It is not necessary to suppose that this Activity emanates from any thing or person *outside* Nature. It may perfectly well exercise its control and guidance from within—just as the activity which is "I" controls, consciously or unconsciously, directly or indirectly, the movements and actions of every particle of which "my" body is made up. But what we cannot but assume is that throughout this prolific and marvellously varied forest life, through every tiny plant and every forest giant, through every leaf and petal, through each little insect and every bird and butterfly, through the wild beasts of the jungle, the wary forest folk, and the most cultured men—through each and all and the whole in its collectedness there runs some kind of unifying Activity, holding the whole together, ordering all, dominating all, directing all—just as the orchid-spirit holds together and directs the activities of each particle which goes to make up the orchid; or the eagle-spirit directs the activities of each particle which goes to make up the eagle.

Suffusing the whole, embracing the whole, permeating each single member of the whole, there must be an organising and directing Activity, or we should not see the order and purposiveness we do.

We shall now see that this Organising Activity gives not only direction, but an *upward* direction to the whole which it controls.

* * *

We have already noted that among individuals the variety is such that no two are exactly alike. Each individual, however nearly alike, varies in some slight degree from every other. And new variations are constantly being created. Now we have to note that besides variation there is *gradation*. There is a *scale* of being. And individuals are graded on that scale. One is higher than another.

As there are gradations in height from the plains to the outlying spurs of the Himalaya, and from these again to the higher ridges, and from these on to the great mountains, and finally to Kinchinjunga and Mount Everest; and as there are gradations in size from tiny plants to the giant trees; so there are gradations in worth and value from the simple lichen or moss to the highly complex orchid; from the microscopic animalculae of a stagnant pond to monkeys and men; from simple primitive men to the highly cultured Bengali; and from the simple Bengali villager to the poet Rabindranath Tagore. Everywhere there is scale, gradation, grade. The differences between individuals is not on the level but on ascending stages. Even in very primitive communities, where all men are equal to the extent that there are no formal chiefs, one or two men always stand out pre-eminently above the rest, above the younger, the less skilful, the less experienced.

There is variation everywhere, and wherever there is variation there is gradation. Living beings are no more exactly *equal* than they are exactly *alike*. Either in proficiency, or in speed, or in strength, or in cunning, or in alertness, or in general worth, one is superior to the other. We determine which is the faster horse by pitting one against the other in a race. We find out which is the superior boxer by making the two men fight each other. We find out which is the cleverest boy by testing him at an examination. We expect to determine which is the ablest political leader by making him submit himself to a General Election. We decide which is the most beautiful rose or orchid by putting the various flowers before a committee of judges. It is seldom possible to say with strict accuracy which one individual is superior to the other, and to arrange the various individuals in their truly right place in the scale. But quite evidently we do recognise the scale and recognise that theoretically it is possible to grade each individual on it, even though our practical methods may be somewhat rough-and-ready.

This fact that gradation, as well as variation, exists is one of the great facts we have to note. For it indicates that the Organising Activity which keeps the individuals together is not keeping them together on a uniform dead level like the ocean, but is propelling them upward like the mountain. The significance of this fact has not hitherto been adequately noted. We are for ever speaking of equality when there is no equality. We have never noted with sufficient attention that everywhere there are grades and degrees. But it is a fact which a contemplation of the forest indelibly impresses on us. And it is a most welcome and inspiring fact, for it gives us a vision of higher things and promotes a zealous emulation among us.

* * *

And the Organising Activity is not only upward-reaching, but forward-looking. It looks to the future. We have remarked how the individuals strive and compete with one another in order to get food and air and light with which to nourish and maintain themselves. But self-maintenance is not their only object. They seek to propagate themselves—to perpetuate their kind. They even make provision for their offspring. They go further still and *sacrifice* themselves that their offspring may flourish.

Here again selfishness is not the last word. Even plants will make provision for their offspring, and in the last resort will sacrifice themselves that their offspring may survive. A plant will fight with its neighbours for the means wherewith to build itself up. But it will also provide for more than mere maintenance. It will build up organs for the purpose of propagating itself. Even ferns have their organs for producing seeds. And many a plant will make a supreme effort to produce offspring rather than die without having perpetuated its kind. And plants—and of course more markedly animals and men—do not stop with merely reproducing their kind. Besides devoting their energies to propagation, they will deliberately make special *provision* for their offspring; they will supply it with albumen and starch. And many insects are not only indefatigable, but highly intelligent, in providing food for their young even before the young are hatched out. They do not lay their eggs on any plant at random, but will wander for miles to find a plant on which their young can feed, and they then lay their eggs on that plant. Individual plants, insects, animals, or men may be frightfully selfish in their hard struggle for existence, but the one thing in regard to which no individual is selfish is in regard to its offspring. Primitive man, utterly callous about the sufferings of animals and of his own fellow-men and even of his wife, is tenderly careful of his child while it remains a child—and this is a very significant trait in his character.

However indifferent the individual may be to the sufferings of those about him, he will make any sacrifice for his offspring. There is some instinct within plants and animals alike which impels them to sacrifice themselves that their kind may continue.

So that Activity which is at the source of all life, and is keeping living things together in an interconnected whole, not only forces them upward in the scale of being, but is also driving them to look forward into the future, to provide for the future—and, indeed, to make the future better than the present.

* * *

This seems to be the way—judging by what we see in the forest—the Activity works. Things have I not come to be as they are by the slap-dash, irresponsible, unregulated methods of mere chance. We cannot fail to see that chance does play *some* part. One seed from a tree may fall into a rivulet and be swept away to the sea, while another may be borne by a gust of wind, or by a bird, on to rich soil where competitors are few, and be able to grow up into a monarch of the forest, to live for a hundred years, and to give birth to thousands like itself. This is true. But chance will not produce the advancement and progress which is observable. Chance will not produce a single one of those organs of adaptation we see in myriads in the forest. And chance would not have made the barren earth of a hundred million years ago bring forth the plant, animal, and human life we see on it to-day.

The Activity does not work on the haphazard methods of pure chance. Nor, on the other hand, are its operations conducted in the rigid, mechanical method of a machine. Nor, again, can the result we see be due to the working of blind physical and chemical processes alone. There is a great deal too much variety and spontaneity and originality about. We could not possibly look upon the forest as a machine—even of the most complicated kind. A machine goes grinding round and round, producing things of exactly the same pattern. Whereas no two things exactly alike are ever turned out in the forest. And blind physical and chemical processes could by *themselves*—by themselves alone—never produce the novelties, the entirely new and unique things, and things higher and higher in the scale of being, which we see in the forest. Only a man impervious to the teaching of common sense could suppose that the care which plant, beast, and man alike show for their offspring could be the result of bare physical and chemical processes without the inclusion with these processes of any other agency whatsoever.

Nor, on the other hand, do we see any signs of the forest being the result of a preconceived plan gradually being worked out—as a bridge is gradually built up according to the previously thought out plan of the engineer. The carrying out of a plan means that in course of time the plan will be completed, and that each stage is a step towards its completion. But in the forest life there is no sign of any beginning of an approach towards the completion of a plan. There is no tendency to a closing in. There is a reaching upward, it is true. But there is also a splaying outward. One line leads up to man. But others splay out to insects, birds, and elephants.

Another noticeable fact is that nowhere is perfection reached. If a plan were being worked we should expect to see the lower stages—like the foundations of the bridge—well and truly laid, incapable of improvement. But no living being—neither the lowliest nor the highest—is itself as a whole or in any one particular absolutely perfect. There is room for improvement everywhere. Most wonderful things we see. But not perfection. The eye is a wonderful thing. But an oculist would point out defects in even the best.

And if it be argued that there has not been sufficient time yet to work out a plan, the reply is that there has been infinite time. Time is infinite. If the Activity were merely working out a plan, the plan would have been completed ages ago.

So the Organising Activity which we see must be working at the back of things, keeping all the separate individuals together in a connected whole, not only preserves the strictest order among them, but grants them freedom, stimulates emulation among them, inspires them to reach upward and to look into and provide for the future. Such an Activity is no mere mechanical activity. It is a purposive Activity. It is an essentially *spiritual* Activity. Spirit is not the casual flash flaming up from the working of blind physical and chemical forces. Spirit dominates these blind forces. Spirit is a true determining factor in the whole process. Spirit is at the root and source and permeates the whole.

This Spiritual Activity is what in ordinary language we speak of as "the Spirit of Nature," and emanates from the Heart of Nature.

* * *

When, therefore, our Artist sums up his impressions of Nature as epitomised in the life of the forest; when he has been able to feel that he has, as it were, got inside the skin of Nature, entered into her Spirit and really understood her—as the artist-midge we have referred to would enter into the nature of a man and try and understand him—he will probably find that Nature works in very much the same way as he himself works, and is of much the same character as himself.

The Artist will observe that Nature neither works by mere chance, tossing up at each turning whether she shall go to the right or to the left, and quite indifferent as to which way she takes; nor in the set and rigid manner of a machine; nor yet, again, in the cut-and-dried fashion which the execution of a previously conceived plan implies. Order everywhere the Artist will have observed. But order need not mean woodenness and machinery. Order is simply the absolutely essential prerequisite of any Freedom. And it is Freedom that the Artist everywhere observes. Nature is not closed in by the designed overarch of an eventually-to-be-completed plan. The zenith and horizon are always open. There is always order, but there is scope illimitable for Nature's workings.

So the sum impression the Artist will probably receive is that Nature is in her essential character an Artist like himself—that she creates and goes on creating, just as he creates and goes on creating. A painter who is a true artist and not a mere copyist paints "out of his head," as the saying goes, pictures which are true creations—something new and unique, though founded on and related to the pre-existing. And there is no limit to the pictures he might paint out of his head. He is not tied down in advance by any preconceived plan. According as he is roused and stirred by the complex life around him, he could—if he were physically able—go on for ever painting picture after picture, each a new creation. In the same way a poet could go on writing poems. The poet does not turn out poems like a machine turns out pins, each like the other. He is not tied down to what he writes. He writes out of his own heart what he likes. And he does not and *could* not turn out two poems exactly the same. Nor does he write according to plan as the bridge-builder works according to the plan of the engineer. He works as he goes. He works by spontaneous creativeness. He is utterly original—a true creator. And even so will our Artist hold that Nature works.

The letters of Nature's alphabet which the Artist sees in the forest are not in the places they are either through mere chance or according to a definitely prepared plan. The letters form words, the words form lines, and the lines form poems. The Artist reads the words and understands the meaning of the poems, and so understands the character of the Poet—the Poet whose name is Nature. But the Artist knows that the words and lines and poems he sees in the forest are there as spontaneous creations from the mind of Nature as poems arise in his own mind. And he knows that Nature could go on—and must go on—creating these poems, painting these pictures, for ever and ever.

Nature will, indeed, work to an end as an Artist works to an end. Nature has purposiveness as an Artist has purposiveness. But that end is something which Nature, like the Artist, is always revising, re-creating, improving, perfecting. An Artist has the general end of creating Beauty, but he is always striving to enrich and intensify it, to create it in greater and greater perfection. And even so does Nature work.

* * *

As the Artist puts himself in touch with the Heart of Nature, the dominant impression he receives is of Nature ever straining after higher, perfection, ever striving to achieve a greater excellence, and create beings with higher and higher, modes of life. He sees her straining upward in the mountain, in the trees, in the climbers on the trees, in every blade of grass. He sees the whole of life, straining to achieve higher and higher forms, more perfect flowers, more intelligent animals, more spiritual men. He sees the life of the seas stretching up out of the seas on to the land. He sees the life of the land striving to reach the highest points on the land. And he sees it also soaring up into the air and making itself at home there, too. Everywhere he sees evidence of aspiration and upward effort.

But he notes also that with this upward effort there goes a downward pull. The mountain strives upward, but it is drawn down by the forces of gravitation. The eagle soars up in the sky, but has to come down to earth to rest and feed. The poet aspires to heaven, but has to stop on earth and earn his daily bread.

Nature, like himself, the Artist finds, is engaged in a constant struggle between an impulse to excentration and the necessity for concentration. She wants to fly off to the zenith and to the horizon, but is continually being drawn into the centre. She wants to let herself go, but has to keep herself in. And all this is to the good. For the necessity for concentration only serves to strengthen and refine her aspiration. And the net result is higher and higher perfection. She cannot rise any higher in a mountain, so she rises in a higher form in a tree. She cannot rise any higher in a tree, so she rises in higher form in an orchid. She cannot rise any higher in an orchid, so she rises in higher form in a man. She cannot rise any higher in man as an intelligent animal, so she rises in higher form in man as a spiritual being, capable of spiritual appreciation and of spiritual communion with her.

The gravitation to a centre—the necessity for concentration—does not suppress and crush the aspiration of Nature; it only serves to compel the aspiration to refine and perfect itself.

In this spirit of aspiration checked by concentration the Artist will surely find what is after his own heart. He will recognise that what is going on in Nature is the same as what goes on in his own heart. He and Nature have a common aspiration. As he aspires but has to concentrate, so does Nature aspire but has to concentrate. As he works, so does Nature work. What he aims at, that also does Nature aim at. And when the Naturalist within him convinces him that, so far as forest life reveals it, this is Nature's manner and this is Nature's end, then his heart goes out to the Heart of Nature, his heart and her heart become one; and from that community of heart Beauty unending springs.

He will without reserve or hesitation be able to throw his whole heart into the enjoyment of Natural Beauty in a way that would have been utterly impossible if he had had to come to the conclusion that Nature cared only for the brutally fittest, wholly irrespective of their worth, or that Nature was at the mercy of chance and had no wish, intention, or power to make good prevail over ill. And with his instinctive love of Natural Beauty thus confirmed and strengthened by this testing of his instinct against what cool reasoning on the facts revealed by observation in the forest had to say about it, he can with lightened heart search still further into Nature, and see her in higher, wider, deeper aspects than the forest alone can disclose.

CHAPTER VI.
KINCHINJUNGA

Aspiration is the root sentiment at the Heart of Nature as she manifests herself in the forest—aspiration upward checked by concentration upon the inmost centre. And the very emblem of the aspiration of Nature kept in hand and under control is to be found in that proud pinnacle of the Sikkim Himalaya, Kinchinjunga, as it is seen from Darjiling rising from amidst the rich tropical forests which clothe its base. To Darjiling, therefore, we should be wise to go.

To reach it we must ascend the slopes of the outer ranges which rise abruptly from the plains. A giant forest now replaces the stunted and bushy timber of the Terai proper and clothes the steep mountain-sides with dense, deep-green, dripping vegetation. The trees are of great height, and are sheathed and festooned with climbing plants of many kinds. Bauhinias and robinias, like huge cables, join tree to tree. Peppers, vines, and convolvulus twine themselves round the trunks and branches, and hang in graceful pendants from the boughs. And the trees, besides being hung with climbers, are also decked with orchids and with foliaceous lichens and mosses. The wild banana with its crown of glistening leaves is everywhere conspicuous. Bamboos shoot up through the undergrowth to a hundred feet or more in height. The fallen trees are richly clothed with ferns typical of the hottest and dampest climates. And dendrobiums and other orchids fasten on the branches.

* * *

At Kurseong there is another striking change, for the vegetation now becomes more characteristic of the temperate zone. The spring here vividly recalls the spring in England. Oaks of a noble species and magnificent foliage are flowering and the birch bursting into leaf. The violet, strawberry, maple, geranium, and bramble appear, and mosses and lichens carpet the banks and roadsides. But the species of these plants differ from their European prototypes, and are accompanied at this elevation (and for 2,000 feet higher up) with tree ferns forty feet in height, bananas, palms, figs, pepper, numbers of epiphytal orchids, and similar genuine tropical genera.

From Kurseong we ascend through a magnificent forest of chestnut, walnut, oaks, and laurels. Hooker, when he subsequently visited the Khasia Hills in Assam, said that though the subtropical scenery on the outer Himalaya was on a much more gigantic scale, it was not comparable in beauty and luxuriance with the really tropical vegetation induced by the hot, damp, and insular climate of those perennially humid Khasia Hills. The forest of gigantic trees on the Himalaya, many of them deciduous, appear from a distance as masses of dark grey foliage, clothing mountains 10,000 feet high. Whereas in the Khasia Hills the individual trees are smaller, more varied in kind, of a brilliant green, and contrast with grey limestone and red sandstone rocks. Still, even of the forest between Kurseong and Darjiling, Hooker says that it is difficult to conceive a grander mass of vegetation—the straight shafts of the timber trees shooting aloft, some naked and clean with grey, pale, or brown bark; others literally clothed for yards with a continuous garment of epiphytes (air-plants), one mass of blossoms, especially the white orchids, coelogynes, which, bloom in a profuse manner, whitening their trunks like snow. More bulky trunks bear masses of interlacing climbers—vines, hydrangea, and peppers. And often the supporting tree has long ago decayed away and their climbers now enclose a hollow. Perpetual moisture nourishes this dripping forest, and pendulous mosses and lichens are met with in profusion.

For this forest life, however, we cannot at present spare the attention that is its due, for we want above all things to see the mountains on the far side of this outer ridge. Tropical forests may be seen in many other parts of the world. But only here on all the Earth can we see mountains on so magnificent a scale. So we do not pause, but cross the ridge and come to the slopes and spurs which face northward, away from the plains and towards the main range of the Himalaya.

Here is situated Darjiling, which ought to be set apart as a sacred place of pilgrimage for all the world. Directly facing the snowy range and set in the midst of a vast forest of oaks and laurels, rhododendrons, magnolias, and camellias, the branches and trunks of which are festooned with vines and smilax and covered with ferns and orchids, and at the base of which grow violets, lobelias, and geraniums, with berberries, brambles, and hydrangeas— it is adapted as few other places are for the contemplation of Nature's Beauty in its most splendid aspects.

Its only disadvantage is that it is so continually shrouded in mist. The range on which it stands being the first range against which the moisture-laden currents from the Bay of Bengal strike, the rainfall is very heavy and amounts to 140 or 160 inches in the year. And even when rain is not actually falling there is much cloud hanging about the mountains. So the traveller cannot count upon seeing the snows. There is no certainty that as he tops the ridge or turns the corner he will see Kinchinjunga in the full blaze of its glory. He cannot be as sure of seeing it as he is of seeing a picture on entering a gallery. During the month of November alone is there a reasonable surety. All the rest of the year he must take his chance and possess his soul in patience till the mountain is graciously pleased to reveal herself.

Perhaps because of the uncertainty of seeing Kinchinjunga the view when it is seen is all the more impressive. The traveller waits for hours and days, even for only a glimpse. One minute's sight of the mountains would satisfy him. But still the clouds eddy about in fleecy billows wholly obscuring the mountains. Six thousand feet below may now and then be seen the silver streak of the Rangit River and forest-clad mountains beyond. Around him are dripping forests, each leaf glistening with freshest greenness, long mosses hanging from the boughs, and the most delicate ferns and noblest orchids growing on the stems and branches. All is very beautiful, but it is the mountain he wants to see; and still the cloud-waves collect and disperse, throw out tender streamers and feelers, disappear and collect again, but always keep a veil between him and the mountain.

Then of a sudden there is a rent in the veil. Without an inkling of when it is to happen or what is to be revealed, those mists of infinite softness part asunder for a space. The traveller is told to look. He raises his eyes but sees nothing. He throws back his head to look higher. Then indeed he sees, and as he sees he gasps. For a moment the current of his being comes to a standstill. Then it rushes back in one thrill of joy. Much he will have heard about Kinchinjunga beforehand. Much he will remember of it if he has seen it before. But neither the expectation nor the memory ever comes up to the reality. From that time, henceforth and for ever, his whole life is lifted to a higher plane.

Through the rent in the fleecy veil he sees clear and clean against the intense blue sky the snowy summit of Kinchinjunga, the culminating peak of lesser heights converging upward to it and all ethereal as spirit, white and pure in the sunshine, yet suffused with the delicatest hues of blue and mauve and pink. It is a vision of colour and warmth and light—a heaven of beauty, love, and truth.

But what really thrills us is the thought that, incredibly high though it is, yet that heaven is part of earth, and may conceivably be attained by man. It is nearly double the height of Mont Blanc and more than six times the height of Ben Nevis, but still it is rooted in earth and part of our own home. This is what causes the stir within us.

Hardly less striking than its height is its purity and serenity. The subtle tints of colour and the brilliant sunlight dispel any coldness we might feel, while the purity is still maintained. And the serenity is accentuated by the ceaseless movements of the eddying clouds through which the vision is seen. There is about Kinchinjunga the calm and repose of stupendous upward effort successfully achieved.

A sense of solemn elevation comes upon us as we view the mountain. We are uplifted. The entire scale of being is raised. Our outlook on life seems all at once to have been heightened. And not only is there this sense of elevation: we seem purified also. Meanness, pettiness, paltriness seem to shrink away abashed at the sight of that radiant purity.

The mountain has made appeal to, and called forth from us all that is most pure and most noble within us, and aroused our highest aspirations. Our heart, therefore, goes out lovingly to it. We long to see it again and again. We long to be always in a mood worthy of it. And we long to have that fineness of soul which would enable us to appreciate it still more fully. Glowing in the heart of the mountain is the pure flame of undaunted aspiration, and it sets something aglow in our hearts also which burns there unquenchably for the rest of our days. We see attainment of the I highest in the physical domain, and it stirs us to achieve the highest in the spiritual. Between ourselves and the mountain is the kinship of common effort towards high ends. And it is because of this kinship that we are able to see such lofty Beauty in the mountain.

For only a few minutes are we granted this heavenly vision. Then the veil is drawn again. But in those few minutes we have received an impression which has gone right down into the depths of our soul and will last there for a lifetime.

* * *

On other occasions the mountain is not so reserved, but reveals itself for whole days in all its glory. The central range of the Himalaya will be arrayed before us in its full majesty from one horizon to the other without a cloud to hide a single detail. We see the lesser ranges rolling up, wave after wave, in higher and higher effort towards the culminating line of peaks. And along this central line itself all the lesser heights we see converging on the supreme peak of Kinchinjunga. The scene, too, will be dazzling in the glorious sunshine and suffused with that purply-blue translucent atmosphere which gives to the whole a fairy-like, ethereal aspect.

And on this occasion we have no hurried glimpse of the mountain. We have ample time to contemplate it, looking at it, turning away from it to rest our souls from so deep an emotion, looking at it again, time after time, till we have entered into its spirit and its spirit has entered into us. And always our eyes insensibly revert to the culminating-point—the summit of Kinchinjunga itself. We note all the rich forest foreground, the deep valley beneath us, the verdure-covered subsidiary ranges, and the strong buttresses of the higher peaks. But our eyes do not linger there. They unconsciously raise themselves beyond them to the summit ridge. Nor do we look long on the distant peaks on either hand. They are over 24,000 feet in height. But they are not the *highest*. So our eyes pass over peaks of every remarkable form—abrupt, rugged, and enticing, and we seek the highest peak of all. And Kinchinjunga is a worthy mountain-monarch. It is not a needle-point—a sudden upstart which might easily be upset. Kinchinjunga is grand and massive and of ample gesture, broad and stable and yet also culminating in a clear and definite point. There is no mistaking her superiority both in massiveness and height to every peak around her.

And thick-mantled in deep and everlasting snow though the whole long range of mountains is, the spectacle of all this snow brings no chill upon us. For we are in latitudes more southern still than Italy and Greece—farther south than Cairo. The entire scene is bathed in warm and brilliant sunshine. The snows are glittering white, but with a white that does not strike cold upon us, for it is tinted in the tenderest way with the most delicate hues of blue and pink. They are, indeed, in the strictest sense not white at all, but a mingling of the very faintest essence of the rose, the violet, and the forget-me-not. And we view the distant mountains through an atmospheric veil which has the strange property of revealing instead of hiding the real nature of the object before which it stands. It does not conceal the mountains. It reveals them in their real nature—the spiritual. Each country has an atmosphere of its own. There is a blue of the Alps, a blue of Italy, a blue of Greece, and a blue of Kashmir. The blue of the Sikkim Himalaya, perhaps on account of the excessive amount of moisture in the air, has a special quality of its own. It seems to me to have more *colour* in it—a *fuller* colour, a bluer blue, a purpler purple than the atmosphere of these other countries. From this cause and from the greater brilliance of the sun there is a more satisfying *warmth* even in the snows.

So besides beauty in the form of the mountains there is this exquisite loveliness of colour. In the immediate foreground are greens, fresh and shining and of every tint. And these shade away into deep purples and violets of the supporting ranges, and these again into those most delicate hues of the snows which vary according to the time of day, from decided rose-pink in the early morning and evening to, perhaps, faintest blue or violet in the full day. And over all and as a background is a sky of the intensest blue. What these colours are it is impossible to describe in words, for even the violet, the rose, and the forget-me-not have not the delicacy which these colours in the atmosphere possess. And assuredly no painter could do them justice, simply because paints and canvas are mediums far too coarse in which to reproduce the impression which such brilliance of light acting on a medium so fine as the thin air produces. The great Russian painter Verestchagin once visited Darjiling, and took his seat to paint the scene. He looked and looked, but did not paint. His wife kept handing him the brush and paints. But time after time he said: "Not now, not now; it is all too splendid." Night came and the picture never was painted. And it never *could* be painted, though great artists most assuredly could at least point out to us in their pictures the subtler glories which are to be seen, and which we expect them to indicate to us.

* * *

So the view of the snows from Darjiling, grand and almost overpowering though it is, has warmth in it too. The main impression is one of magnitude and amplitude, of vastness and immensity, and withal of serene composure. The first view of the mountain seen through a rent in the clouds was perhaps more uplifting, though this view excites a sense of elevation also, for the eye is continually being drawn to the highest point. But in this full view the impression of breadth and bigness of scale is combined with the impression of height. The *dimensions* of life in every direction seem to be enlarged. We seem to be able to look at things from a broader, bigger point of view, as well as a higher. We ourselves and the world at large are all on a larger scale than we had hitherto suspected. And while on a broader scale, we feel that things are always working *upward* and converging towards some lofty but distinct, defined summit. This also do we feel, as we look upon the view, that with all the bigness and massiveness and loftiness there is the very finest tenderness as well—such delicacy as we had never before imagined.

And to anyone who really knows them the littleness of man in comparison with these mighty mountains is not the impression made upon him. He is not overawed and overcome by them. His soul goes out most lovingly to them because they have aroused in him all the greatness in his soul, and purified it—even if only for a time—of all its dross and despicableness. And he loves them for that. He does not go cringing along, feeling himself a worm in comparison with them. There is warm kinship between him and them. He knows what is in their soul. And they have aroused in his soul exactly what he rejoices in having aroused there, and which but for them might have remained for ever unsurmised. So he revels in their Beauty.

* * *

Another aspect in which we may see Kinchinjunga is in its aspect at dawn. It will be still night—a starlit night. The phantom snowy range and the fairy forms of the mountains will be bathed in that delicate yellow light the stars give forth. The far valley depths will be hidden in the sombrest purple. Overhead the sky will be glittering with brilliant gems set in a field of limpid sapphire. The hush of night will be over all—the hush which heralds some great and splendid pageant.

Then, almost before we have realised it, the eastward-facing scarps of the highest peaks are struck with rays of mingled rose and gold, and gleam like heavenly realms set high above the still night-enveloped world below. Farther and farther along the line, deep and deeper down it, the flush extends. The sapphire of the sky slowly lightens in its hue. The pale yellow of the starlight becomes merged in the gold of dawn. White billowy mists of most delicate softness imperceptibly form themselves in the valley depths and float up the mountain-sides. The deep hum of insect life, the chirping of the birds, the sounds of men, begin to break the hush of night. The snows become a delicate pink, the valleys are flooded with purple light, the sky becomes intensest blue, and the sun at last itself appears above the mountains, and the ardent life of day vibrates once more.

In the full glare of day the mountains are not seen at their very best. The best time of all to see them is in the evening. If we go out a little from Darjiling into the forest to some secluded spur we can enjoy an evening of rare felicity. On the edge of the spur the forest is more open. The ground is covered with grass and flowers and plants with many-coloured leaves. Rich orchids and tender ferns and pendant mosses clothe the trees. Graceful vines and creepers festoon themselves from bough to bough. The air is fragrant with the scent of flowers. Bright butterflies flutter noiselessly about. The soft purr of forest life drones around. Rays from the setting sun slant across the scene. The leaves in their freshest green and of every shade glitter like emeralds in the brilliant light.

Through the trunks of the stately trees and under their overarching boughs we look out towards the snowy mountains. We look over the brink of the spur, down into the deeps of the valleys richly filled with tropical vegetation, their eastward-facing sides now of purplest purple, their westward-facing slopes radiant in the evening sunshine, with the full richness of their foliage shown up by the dazzling light. Far below we see the silver streak of some foaming river, and then as we raise our eyes we mark ridge rising behind ridge, higher and higher and each of a deeper shade of purple than the one in front. The lower are still clothed in forest, but the green has been merged in the deep purple of the atmosphere. The higher are bare rock till the snow appears. But just across them floats a long level wisp of fleecy cloud, and apparently the limits of earth have been reached and sky has begun. We would rest content with that. But our eyes are drawn higher still. And high above the cloud, and rendered inconceivably higher by its presence, emerges the snowy summit of Kinchinjunga, serene and calm and flushed with the rose of the setting sun. As a background is a sky of the clearest, bluest blue.

These are the chief elements of the scene, but all is in process of incessant yet imperceptible change. The sunshine slowly softens, the purples deepen, the flush on the mountains reddens. The air becomes as soft as velvet. Not a leaf now stirs. A holy peace steals over the mountains and settles in the valleys. The snow mountains no longer look cold, hard, and austere. Their purity remains as true as ever. And they still possess their uplifting power. But they now speak of serenity and calm—not, indeed, of the unsatisfying ease of the slothful, but of the earned repose of high attainment. Great peace is about them—deep, strong, satisfying peace.

The sun finally sets. Night has settled in the valleys. The lights of Darjiling sparkle in the darkness. But long afterwards a glow still remains on Kinchinjunga. Lastly that also fades away. And now night spreads her veil on every part. But here night brings with it no sense of gloom and darkness, much less death. Far otherwise, for now it seems as if we were only beginning our intenser and still wider life. The fret of ordinary life is soothed away in the serene ending of the day. The quietness, profound and meaningful, yet further calms our spirit. Every condition is now favourable for the life of that inmost soul of us, which is too sensitive often to emerge into the glare and rubs of daylight life, but which in this holy peace, in the presence of the heavenly mountains, and with the stars above to guide it, can reach out to its fullest extent and indulge its highest aspirations.

CHAPTER VII.
HIGH SOLITUDES

From these scenes of tropical luxuriance and teeming life I would transport the Artist to a region of austerest beauty, far at the back of the Himalaya, where only one white man as yet has penetrated: where no life at all exists—no tree, no simplest plant, no humblest animalcula; where, save for some rugged precipice too steep for snow to lie, and save also for the intense azure of the sky, all is radiant whiteness. A region far distant from any haunt of man, where reigns a mountain which acknowledges supremacy to Mount Everest alone. A region of completest solitude, where the solemn silence is unbroken by the twitter of a single bird or the drone of the smallest insect, and is disturbed only by the occasional thunder of an avalanche or the grinding crunch of the glacier as a reminder of the titanic forces which are perpetually though invisibly at work.

Freezing this region is and full of danger. And there is no short cut to it and no easy means of transport. Only men in the prime of health can reach there and return. And it is only men whose faculties are at their finest who are fit to stand the austerity of its cold, stern beauty. It lies at the dividing line between India and Central Asia where the waters which flow to India are parted from the waters which flow to Central Asia, and where the Indian and Chinese Empires touch one another. It may be approached from two directions—from Turkistan or from Kashmir and the Karakoram Pass. The Artist had better approach it by Kashmir, for he will see there certain beauties which even Sikkim does not possess, and this will make him further realise the variety of beauty this earth displays.

Kashmir is altogether different from Sikkim. In Sikkim the valleys are deep, steep, and narrow, and markedly inclined, so that the rivers run strong and there is no room or level for lakes. In Kashmir the main valley is from twenty to thirty miles broad and ninety miles long. Over a large portion it is nearly dead level. So the river is even and placid. And there are tranquil lakes and duck-haunted marshes.

The climate is different, too. It is the climate of North Italy. Consequently there are no tropical forests, and the mountain-sides are covered with trees of the temperate zone—the stately deodar cedars, spruce fir, maples, walnut, sycamore, and birch; while in the valley itself grow poplars, willows, mulberries, and most beautiful of all, and a speciality of Kashmir, the magnificent chenar tree—akin to the plane tree of Europe, but larger, fuller, and richer in its foliage.

In Kashmir there is also far more variety of colour than there is in Sikkim. And in the spring, with the willows and poplars in freshest green; the almond, pear, apple, apricot, and peach trees in full blossom, white and pink; the fields emerald with young wheat, blue with linseed, or yellow with mustard; and the village-borders purple with iris; or in the autumn when the chenars, the poplars, and apricots are turning to every tint of red and yellow and purple, Kashmir is in a glow of colour. And the famous Valley is all the more beautiful because it is ringed round with a circle of snowy mountains of at least Alpine magnitude, with a glimpse here and there, such as that of Nanga Parbat, of much more stupendous peaks beyond; and because the sky is so blue, the atmosphere so delicate in its hues, and the sunshine so general throughout the year.

In this favoured land there is many a variety of beauty, but all is of the easy, pleasant kind. All the colours are soft and soothing. It is a land to dream of, a gentle and indulgent land of soft repose, and calm content, and quiet relaxation; a dreamy, peaceful land where life glides smoothly forward, and all makes for enjoyment and idleness and holiday.

From the pleasant Vale of Kashmir the Artist would have to make his way up the Sind Valley—a valley, typical of those beautiful tributaries which add so much to the whole charm of Kashmir. These are comparatively narrow, and the mountain-sides are steep, but the valleys are not so narrow nor the sides so steep as the valleys of Sikkim, nor are the forests anything like so dense. The scenery is, indeed, much more Swiss in appearance with open pine forests, picturesque hamlets, grassy pasture-lands, flowery meadows, and clear, rushing rivers; and with the rocky crests or snow-capped summits of the engirdling mountains always in the background.

But when we emerge from this delightful valley of the Sind River and cross the Zoji-la Pass, we come upon a very different style of country—bare, dreary, desolate, monotonous, uninteresting. The forest has all disappeared, for the rainfall is here slight. The moisture-laden clouds have precipitated themselves upon the seaward-facing slopes of the mountains we have already passed through. And because of this lack of rainfall the valleys are not cut out deep, but are high and broad. It is a delightful experience to pass from this brown, depressing landscape to the rich beauties of the Sind Valley and Kashmir. But to make the journey the other way round, and to pass *into* the gloomy region after being spoilt by the luxuries of Kashmir, is sadly disheartening at first.

The experience has, however, its advantages, for it makes us throw off all ideas of soft ease we may have harboured in Kashmir, and reminds us that we have to prepare ourselves to face beauties of a far sterner kind. So we insensibly alter our whole attitude of mind, and as we plod our way through the mountains we summon up from within ourselves all the austerer stuff of which we are made.

We cross some easy passes of 13,000 feet or so in height. We cross the River Indus. We reach Leh. We cross a 17,000 feet pass and then a glacier pass of 18,000 feet, and then the watershed of India and Central Asia by the Karakoram Pass, nearly 19,000 feet in height. We are six hundred miles from the plains of India now, and in about as desolate a region as the world contains. Then, bearing westward, we make for the Aghil Pass. We have now got right in behind the Himalaya, and as we reach the top of the Aghil Pass we look towards the Himalaya from the Central Asian side, on what is known as the Karakoram Range, and here at last is the remote, secluded glacier region which has been the object of our search.

Its glory bursts upon us as we top the last rise to the Aghil Pass. Across the deep valley is arrayed in bold and jagged outline a series of pinnacles of ice glistening in the brilliant sunshine, showing up in clearest definition against the intense blue sky, and rising abruptly and incredibly high above the rock-bound Oprang River. They are the mighty peaks which group around K2— the noblest cluster in the whole Himalaya.

There are here no inviting grassy slopes and no enticing forests. The mountain-sides are all hard rock and rugged precipices. And the summits are of ice or with edges sharp and keen direct from Nature's workshop. But the sight, though it awes us, does not depress us or deter us. We are keyed up by high anticipation when we arrive on the threshold of this secluded region, and a fierce joy seizes us as we first set eyes on these mountains. We know we have before us one of the great sights of the world—something unique and apart, something the like of which we shall never see again. And awed as we are by the mountains' unsurpassed magnificence, we do not bow down in any abject way before them. We are not impressed by our littleness in comparison. They have, indeed, shown us that the world is something greater than we knew. But they have shown us also that *we* too are something greater than we knew. The peaks in their dazzling altitude have set an exacting standard for us. They have incited us to rise to that standard. Their call is great, but a thrill runs through us as we feel ourselves responding to the challenge, collecting ourselves together and gathering up every stiffest bit of ourselves to rise to their high standard. We feel nerved and steeled; and in high exhilaration we plunge down into the valley to join issue with the mountains.

Arrived on the Oprang River we can turn either to the left or the right. If we turn to the left we get right in under a knot of stupendous peaks. Towering high and solitary above the rocky wall which bounds the valley on the south is a peak which may be K2, 28,250 feet in height, which must be somewhere in the neighbourhood. But the investigations of the Duke of the Abruzzi throw a doubt as to whether this can be K2 itself. If it is not, it must be some unfixed and unnamed peak. At any rate it is a magnificent, upstanding peak rising proud and steep-sided high and clear above its neighbours. Then beyond it, farther up the Oprang Valley, we catch glimpses of that wondrous company of Gusherbrum Peaks—four of them over 26,000 feet in height, with rich glaciers flowing from them.

But if we turn to the right on descending from the Aghil Pass, and if we turn again in the direction of the Mustagh Pass, we come to an icy realm which has about it, above every other region, the impress of both extreme remoteness and loftiest seclusion. As we ascend right up the glacier—either the one coming down from the Mustagh Pass or the one to the east running parallel with the general line of the Karakoram Range—we feel not only far away from but also high above the rest of the world. And we seem to have risen to an altogether purer region. Especially if we sleep in the open, without any tent, with the mountains always before us, with the stars twinkling brightly above us, do we have this sense of having ascended to a loftier and serener world.

At the heads of these glaciers there is little else but snow and ice. The moraines have almost disappeared—or, rather, have hardly yet come into being. And the mountains are so deeply clothed in ice and snow, it is only when they are extremely steep that rock appears. The glacier-filled valley below and the mountain above are therefore almost purely white. The atmosphere, too, is marvellously clear, so that by day the mountains and glaciers glitter brightly in the sunshine, and at night the stars shine out with diamond brilliance. The effect on a moonlight night is that of fairyland. We see the mountains as clearly as we would by the daylight of many regions, but the light is now all silver, and the mountains not solid and substantial but ethereal as in a vision.

The pureness of the beauty is unspotted. It is the direct opposite of the voluptuous beauty of Kashmir. No one would come here for repose and holiday. But we like to have been there once. We like to have attained even once in a lifetime to a world so refined and pure.

Cold it may be—and dangerous. But we soon forget the cold. And the dangers only string us up to meet them, so that we are in a peculiarly alert, observant mood. And we have a secret joy in watching Nature in her most threatening aspects and in measuring ourselves against her.

White it may be, but not colourless. For the whiteness of the snow is most exquisitely tinged with blue. The lakelets on the glacier are of deepest blue. They are encircled by miniature cliffs of ice of transparent green. The blueness of the sky is of a depth only seen in the highest regions. And the snowy summits of the mountains are tinged at sunset and dawn with finest flush of rose and primrose. So with all the whiteness there is, too, the most delicate colouring.

Standing thus on the glacier and looking up to the snowy peaks all round us, we think how, wholly unobserved by men, they have reared themselves to these high altitudes and there remain century by century unseen by any human being. From deep within the interior of the earth they have arisen. And they are only touched by the whitest snowflakes. They are only touched by snowflakes fashioned from the moisture which the sun's rays have raised off the surface of the Indian Ocean, and which the monsoon winds have transported in invisible currents, high above the plains of India, till they are gently precipitated on these far-distant heights.

"Blessed are the pure in heart," we are told, "for they shall see God." And blessed are they who are able to ascend to a region like this, for here they cannot but be pure in heart, and cannot *help* seeing God. For the time being at least, they *have* to be pure. In the spotless purity of that region they cannot harbour any thought that is sordid or unclean. And they pray that ever after they may maintain what they have reached. For they know that if they could maintain it they would see beauties which in the murky state of common life it is impossible to perceive. In the white purity which this high region exacts they are forced to pierce through the superficial and unimportant and they catch sight of the real.

They are in a remote and lofty solitude, and in touch with the naked elementals of which the world has built itself. But they do not feel alone. They feel themselves in a great Presence, and in a Presence with which they are most intimately in touch. And it is no dread Presence, but one which they delight to feel. Holiness is its essence, and their souls are purged and purified. They are suffused with it; it enters deeply into them, and translates them swiftly upward.

CHAPTER VIII.
THE HEAVENS

The remote glacier region gives us a sense of purity, and gives us, too, a vision of colour in its finest delicacy. But for depth, extent, and brilliancy of colour we must look to sunsets—and sunsets in those high desert regions where the outlook is widest and the atmosphere clearest.

In deserts everywhere marvellous sunsets may be seen, for the comparative absence of moisture in the atmosphere and the presence of invisible particles of dust gives these sunsets an especial brilliancy. In the middle of the day a desert in its uniform brownness is dreary and monotonous to a degree. But at dawn and sunset when the sun's rays slant across the scene the desert glows with colour of every shade and hue and in ever-changing combination. In the Gobi Desert of Central Asia, in the Egyptian Desert, in the Arabian Desert, in Arizona, I have seen sunsets that thrill one with delight. But nowhere have I seen more glorious sunsets than in the highlands of Tibet. And what makes them there so remarkable is that the plains themselves are 15,000 feet above sea-level, so that the atmosphere is exceptionally clear. Great distances are therefore combined with unusual clearness. The country is open enough and the air clear enough for us to see far distances. And extent is a prime essential in the glory of a sunset.

It is difficult to make those who have never been outside Europe understand what sunsets can be. In England, as Turner has shown, there are sunsets to be seen containing in abundance many such elements of beauty as varied and varying and great extent of colour. But the atmosphere here is so thick that the colours appear as if thrown on to a solid background. So the sunsets look opaque. On the continent of Europe the atmosphere is clearer and the opaqueness less pronounced. The colouring is in consequence more vivid. But—except in high Alpine regions—the clearness does not approach the clearness of Tibet. And neither in England nor on the Continent do we get the great *distances* of desert sunsets. And great distances increase immeasurably that feeling of *infinity* which is the chief glory in a sunset.

The clearness of the atmosphere is important in this respect also, that it produces the effect upon the colours of the sunset that they seem more like the colours we see in precious stones than the colours a painter throws on a canvas. There is no milkiness or murkiness in them. The sky is so clear that we see a colour as we see the red in a ruby. We see deep into the colour. The colour comes right *out* of the sky and has not the appearance of being merely plastered on the surface.

And the variety of the colours and the rapidity with which they change and merge and mingle into one another is another wonder of these desert sunsets. It would be wholly impossible to paint a picture of them which would adequately express the impression they give, for the main impression is derived from light, and the colours are therefore far more glowing than they could ever be reproduced on canvas. Nor can the changing effects be reproduced on a stationary medium. The nearest approach to the glory of a Tibet sunset which I have seen is a picture in pastel by Simon de Bussy a sunset in the Alps. But all pictures—even Turner's;—can only draw attention to the glory and show us what to look for. They cannot reproduce the impression in full. The medium through which the artist has to work—the paints and the canvas—are inadequate for his needs.

If we try to describe the impression in words we are no better off. We can, indeed, compare the sunset colours with the colours of flowers and precious stones. But here also we miss the light which is the very foundation of the sunset beauties. And we have neither the changefulness nor the vast extent of the sunset colouring.

To get the least idea of the variety of colours mixing, merging, and intermingling with one another we must go to the opal, though even there there is not the intensity of colour, and of course not the change nor extent. From an orange—especially a blood orange—we get a notion of the combined reds and yellows of the sunsets, though the reds may range deeper than orange into the reds of the ruby or the cardinal flower, and lighter into the pinks of the rose or the carnation; and the yellows range from the gold of the eseholtzia to the delicate hue of the primrose. And for the translucency of their yellower effects we must bring in the amber. Often there is a green which can only be matched by jade or emerald. And sometimes there is an effect with which only the amethyst can be compared. Then there are mauves and purples for which the precious stones have no parallel, and of which heliotrope, the harebell, and the violet give us the best idea. And the blues range from the deep blue of the sapphire and the gentian to the light blue of the turquoise and the forget-me-not.

In these stones and flowers we get something near the actual colour, but the depth, the clearness, the luminosity, and the vast extent are all wanting, and these are all essential features of the sunset's glories. So we must imagine all these colours glowing with light and never still—perpetually changing from one to the other and shading off from one into the other, one colour emerging, rising to the dominant position, and then disappearing to give place to another, and effecting these changes imperceptibly yet rapidly also, for if we take our eyes away for even a few minutes we find that the aspect has altogether altered.

From my camp in Tibet for weeks together I could be sure of witnessing every evening one of these glorious sunsets. For while the mighty monsoon clouds used to roll up on to the line of Himalayan peaks and pile themselves up there, billow upon billow, in magnificent array, dark and fearful in the general mass, but clear-edged and silver-tipped along the summits, yet beyond that line, in Tibet, the sky was nearly always clear and blue of the bluest. With nothing whatever to impede my view—no trees, nor houses, nor fences, nor obstacles of any kind—I could look out far over these open plains to distant hills; beyond them, again, to Mount Everest a hundred miles away; beyond it, again, to still more distant mountains; and, finally, behind them into the setting sun. And these far hills and snowy mountains, seen as they were across an absolutely open plain, seemed not to impede the view but only to heighten the impression of great distance. The eye would be led on from feature to feature, each receding farther into the distance till it seemed only a step from the farthest snowy mountain into the glowing sun itself.

Every evening, whenever I could, I used to walk out alone into the open plain to feast my soul on the splendid scene. In the stern glacier region round K2 had had to brace myself up and to summon up all that was toughest within me in order to cope with the terribly exacting conditions in which I found myself. In the presence of these calm but fervent sunsets there was a different feeling. I had a sense of expansion, a longing to let myself go. And I would feel myself craving to let myself go out all I could into these glowing depths of light and colour, and trying to open myself out to their beauty, that as much as possible of it should flow into me and glorify my whole being. I had the feeling that in those sunsets there was *any* length for my soul to go out to—that there was *infinite* room there for the soul's expansion. There was inexhaustible glory for the soul to absorb, and the soul was thirsting for it and could never have enough.

Evening after evening came to me, too—quite unconsciously, and as it were inevitably—Shelley's words (slightly altered):

> "Be thou, spirit bright,
>> My spirit! Be thou me, most glorious one!
>> Be through my lips to unawakened earth
>> The trumpet of a prophecy."

It was not that there was any particular message that I had to give. But there was aroused in me just this simple, insistent longing to let others know what glory there was in the world, and to be able to communicate to them something of the joy I was then feeling in beholding it. I was highly privileged in having this opportunity of witnessing a Tibetan sunset's splendours. I was yearning for others to share my enjoyment with me.

The white radiance of the glacier region instils into us a sense of purity, and without the purity of heart which that stern region exacts we cannot see the sunset's glory in all its fulness. But now in these Tibetan sunsets we have not purity alone, but warmth and richness as well. They give an impression of infinity of glory. We catch alight from their consuming glory, and our hearts flame up in correspondence with them. The fervent glow in the Heart of Nature kindles a like glow in our own hearts; and we are enraptured by the Beauty.

On our misty island we are apt to connect sunsets with coming darkness and a black end of things. And in gazing on them we are prone to have a sense of sadness mingled with our joy. They seem to mean for us a passage from light to darkness, and from life to death.

But in the deserts we have no such feeling. As day imperceptibly fades away it is not black darkness that succeeds, but a light that enables us to see farther, a mellower light that enables us to see the Universe at large. From this earthly life we are transported to a higher, intenser, ampler life among the stars.

And it is in the desert that we best live among the stars. In Europe we look up into the sky between trees and houses; and among the clouds and through a murky atmosphere we see a few stars. Even when we have a clear sky we seldom get a chance of seeing the whole expanse of the heavens all the way round. And even if we get this rare chance of a clear sky and a wide horizon we do not live with the stars in the open the night through and night after night.

In the Gobi Desert I had this precious opportunity. And I had it when my whole being was tuned up to highest pitch. I was not in the limp state of one who steps out into his garden and looks up casually to the stars. I was tense with high enterprise. I was passing through unknown country on a journey across the Chinese Empire from Peking to India. I was keen and alive in every faculty, in a state of high exhilaration, and both observant and receptive. It was a rare chance, and much I wish now I had made more of it.

My party in crossing the Gobi Desert consisted only of a Chinese guide, a Chinese servant, and a Mongol camel-man. As I had no European companion

I was driven in upon myself. I had to explore a route never before traversed by Europeans, and the distance to be covered across the open steppes of Mongolia and over the Gobi Desert to the first town in Turkestan was twelve hundred miles. Beyond that was the whole length of Turkestan and the six-hundred-mile breadth of the Himalaya to be crossed before I should reach India. So I had a big task before me, and was stirring with the sense of high adventure and vast distances to overcome.

To enable my eight camels to feed by daylight, I used to start at five o'clock in the afternoon and march till one or two in the morning. Sometimes in order to reach water we had to march all through the night and well into the following day. Frequently there were terrific sandstorms, but there were seldom any clouds. So the atmosphere was clear. In the distance were sometimes hills. But for the most part all round the desert was absolutely open. I could see for what seemed an indefinite distance in any direction. The conditions were ideal for observing the stars.

Seated on my camel, or trudging along apart from my little caravan, I would watch the sun set in always varying splendour. No two sunsets were anything like the same. Each through the ascendancy of some one shade of colour, or through an unusual combination of colour, had a special beauty of its own. I would watch each ripening to the climax and then shade away into the beauty of the night. And when the day was over the night would reveal that higher, wider life which daylight only served to hide.

The sunset glow would fade away. Star after star would spring into sight till the whole vault of heaven was glistening with diamond points of light. Above me and all round me stars were shining out of the deep sapphire sky with a brilliance only surpassed by the stars in the high Himalayan solitudes I have already described. And a great stillness would be over all—a silence even completer than the silence among the mountains, for there it was often broken by creaking of the ice, whereas here in the desert it was so profound that, when at the end of many weeks I arrived at a patch of grass and trees, the twittering of the birds and the whirr of insects sounded like the roar of a London street.

In this unbroken stillness and with the eye free to rove all round with nothing in any direction to stay its vision, and being as I was many weeks' distance from any settled human habitation, I often had the feeling of being more connected with the starry firmament than with this Earth. In a curious way the bodily and the material seemed to exist no longer, and I would be in spirit among the stars. They served to guide us over the desert and I gradually became familiar with them. And I used to feel as much a part of the Stellar World as of this Earth. I lost all sense of being confined to Earth and took my place in the Universe at large. My home was the whole great Cosmos before me. The Cosmos, and not the Earth, was the whole to which I belonged.

And in that unbroken quiet and amid this bright company of heaven my spirit seemed to become intenser and more daring. Right high up in the zenith, to infinite height, it would soar unfettered. And right round to any distance in any direction it would pierce its way. The height and distance of the highest and farthest stars I knew had been measured. I knew that the resulting number of miles is something so immense as to be altogether beyond human conception. I knew also that the number of stars, besides those few thousands which I saw, had to be numbered in hundreds of millions. All this was astonishing, and the knowledge of it filled me with wonder at the immensity of the Starry Universe. But it was not the mere magnitude of this world that impressed me. What stirred me was the Presence, subtly felt, of some mighty all-pervading Influence which ordered the courses of the heavenly hosts and permeated every particle.

We cannot watch the sun go down day after day, and after it has set see the stars appear, rise to the meridian and disappear below the opposite horizon in regular procession, without being impressed by the order which prevails. We feel that the whole is kept together in punctual fashion, and is not mere chaos and chance. The presence of some Power upholding, sustaining, and directing the whole is deeply impressed upon us. And in this Presence so steadfast, so calm, so constant, we feel soothed and steadied. The frets and pains of ordinary life are stilled. Deep peace and satisfaction fill our souls.

Sandstorms so terrific that we cannot stand before them or see a thing a foot or two distant come whirling across the desert, and all for the time seems turmoil and confusion and nothing is visible. But behind all we know the stars still pursue their mighty way. At the back of everything we realise there is a Power constant and dependable in whom we can absolutely put our trust.

This is the impression—the impression of steadfastness, constancy, and reliability—which a nightly contemplation of the stars makes upon us. At the foundation of things is something dependable, something in which we can repose our faith. And so the sense of calm and confidence we feel.

And in the desert we have no feeling that the stars pursue their course in cold indifference to us—that the Power which sustains them works its soulless way unregardful of the frettings of us little men. Not thus are we who watch the desert stars impressed. Quite otherwise. For nowhere do we feel the Influence nearer, more intimate or more beneficent. We seem in the very midst of the great Presence. We are immersed in it. It is pervading us on every side. We do not expect it to alter the whole course of Nature for our private good. But we feel confident that the course of Nature is for *good*—that

Nature is a beneficent and no callous Power, and has good at heart. *Because* the foundations are so sure and good we can each pursue our way in confidence. This is the impression we get.

And the Power which guides the stars upon their heavenly way, and which, in guiding them, guides us across the desert, does not reside, we feel, in lonely grandeur in the empty places of the heavens, but in the stars themselves—in their very constitution—in each individually and in all in their togetherness. It burns in each star and shines forth from it, and yet holds the whole together as we see it every night in that circling vault around us. The Activity does not appear to us to emanate from some Invisible Being dwelling wholly apart and isolated from the stars and this Earth, and sending forth invisible spiritual rays, as the Sun stands apart from the Earth but sends out rays of sunlight to it. It seems rather to dwell in the very heart and centre of each star, and the stars seem *spiritual* rather than material beings. So this Power, as we experience it in the desert, does not impress us as being awful and remote, gloomy and inexorable, enforcing unbending law and exacting terrible penalties. Our impression of it is that, though it preserves order with unfailing regularity, it is yet near and kindly, radiating with light and warmth. We not only feel it to be something steadfast, something on which we can rely and in which we may have confidence; we also feel warmed and kindled by it.

So what we get from a nightly contemplation of the stars is a sense of happy companionship with Nature. The Heart of Nature as here revealed is both dependable and kindly. Nature is our friend. And in her certain friendship the balm of peace falls softly on us. Our hearts blend tenderly with the Heart of Nature; and in their union we see Beauty of the gentlest and most reassuring kind.

CHAPTER IX.
HOME BEAUTY

The Artist in his quest for Natural Beauty will have pursued it in the remotest and wildest parts of the Earth, where he can see Nature in her primeval and most elemental simplicity. He will have seen her in many and most varied aspects—the grandest, the wildest, and the most luxuriant. And from these numerous and so different manifestations of Nature he will have been enabled more fully to understand her meaning and comprehend her soul. Moreover, this contemplation of Nature will have evoked from within himself much that he had never suspected he possessed, and thereby his own soul also he will have learned to understand. And from this completer comprehension of his own soul and hers will have emerged a fuller community of heart between him and Nature. He will have come to worship her with a still more ardent devotion, and through the intensity of his love discovered richer and richer Beauty in her.

But even yet he has not seen Natural Beauty where it can be found in its highest perfection. Only when there can be the most intimate possible relationship between him and the natural object he is contemplating can Beauty at its finest be seen. And this closest correspondence of all between him and Nature will only be when he is in the natural surroundings with which he has been familiar from childhood, and which have affected him in his most impressionable years.

The Artist will have seen Nature as she manifests herself in the teeming life of a tropical forest and the most varied races of men; in the highest mountains and the widest deserts; in the glory of sunsets and the calm of stars. But it is in none of these that he will see deepest into the true Heart of Nature and understand her best. It is amid scenery which he has loved since boyhood, in the hearts of his own countrymen in their own country, that he will see deepest into Nature. And deepest of all will he see when from among his countrywomen he has united himself to the one of his own deliberate choice, and in this union realised in its fulness, strength, and intensity that Creative Love which springs from Nature's very heart, and is the ultimate fount and source of all Natural Beauty.

We like to go out over all the Earth and see the wonders of it. And we learn to love the great mountains and rich forests and unfenced steppes and veldts and prairies. And we get to love also the various peoples among whom we have to work and travel. But in his heart of hearts each man likes to get back to the scenes of his childhood. The plainsman likes to get back again from the mountains to his level plains where the scene is closer and more intimate. The mountaineer likes to retire again from the plains into the mountains. The dweller on the veldt likes to get out of the forest on to the great open spaces once more. The inhabitant of the forest likes to get back there again from the plains. And the Englishman, though he loves the Alps and the Himalaya, is touched by nothing so deeply as by a Devonshire lane with its banks of primroses and violets. And he may have the greatest affection for peoples of other races among whom he may have had to work, yet it is his own countrymen that he will always really love.

So the Artist comes back to home surroundings and his own people. And he will return with his sense of beauty quickened and refined by this wide and varied experience of Nature. His sensibility to the beauties of Nature will now be of rarest delicacy, and his capacity for fine discrimination and his feeling for distinction and excellence sure and keen.

He will have been toned and tuned up to the highest pitch in his wrestling with Nature, and will have been purged and purified in the white region of the highest mountains. And in this high-strung state he will now see that creation and manifestation of Nature which of all natural objects will best declare her meaning, bring him into closer touch with her very Heart, and stir in him the deepest emotions. Between him and this object there will be possible the closest community of soul. Here then he will see Natural Beauty at its very finest.

The natural object in which he will see this consummation of Beauty will be the woman who will be to him a kindred spirit, and whom he will first admire and then love.

It was through the love of man and woman for each other in the far-off ages when love first came into the hearts of men that Natural Beauty also first dawned upon them. It is through that love that Natural Beauty has been continually growing in fulness and splendour. And it will be through that same love of man and woman for each other that the Artist will see Natural Beauty reach its highest perfection. For in this love man first learned to enter into the soul of another, to recognise samenesses between himself and another, and to live in communion with another. And so in time he came to recognise samenesses between what was in his heart and what was in the Heart of Nature, to enter into communion with Nature, and through the wedding of himself with Nature see the Beauty in her. He was able in some slight degree to be towards Nature what we see the midge buzzing round a man must be if that midge is to see the beauty of man. Just as the midge, if it is to see the beauty in man, must be able to recognise samenesses between its life and the life of man, so man to see Beauty in Nature had to recognise identity of life between him and Nature as he was first inspired to see it through the love of man and woman for each other. And now the Artist with his wide experience of Nature and united with his own countrywoman in his own country will recognise a still closer identity between himself and Nature, and so see an even fuller Beauty in her.

Assuming the man and woman, both by their upbringing and by outward circumstances, to have been able to develop the best capacities within them and to be meeting now under conditions most favourable for their union, we shall see how perfect is the Beauty which may be revealed. The man will be in the prime of his manhood, and the woman in the prime of her womanhood. The man manly and radiating manhood, the woman womanly and radiating womanhood: their manhood and womanhood welling up within them, each eager to answer the call of the other.

Hers will be no light and shallow beauty insipid as milk and water, but will be sweet as the violet, delicate as the primrose, pure as the lily, yet with all the sweetness, delicacy and purity, radiant as the sunrise. And they will be no pale and puny lovers, soft and mild as doves, and content to lead a dull and trivial life. They will be high of spirit, graceful, swift, and supple as the greyhound; and as keenly intent on living a full and varied life with every moment of it worth while as ever the greyhound is in pursuing its object. They will be capable of intense and passionate emotion, yet with all their eager impulsiveness they will have wills strong to keep themselves in hand, and to maintain their direction true through all the mazy intricacies of life and love.

In the bringing together of such a pair Natural Beauty will play a vitally important part. Of all objects that Nature has produced—of all the offspring of the Earth—such a man and woman are the most beautiful. And we may assume that as they are drawn to each other they will put forth the very best of themselves and give out the utmost beauty that is in them. Moreover, they will be more beautiful to each other than they are to anybody else. Unconsciously they will reveal to each other what they *can* reveal to none other but themselves. Insensibly the windows of their souls will be opened to each other. The lovelight in their eyes—the lovelight which can *only* be shown to each other—will discover to them hidden depths of beauty they had never gathered they possessed.

And this beauty will be something more than mere prettiness or handsomeness of face. The man will see the beauty of the woman—and she his—not only in the face and features, but in the presence, bearing, and carriage, in the gestures, movements, and behaviour. Behind the outward aspect he will see the inward spirit, the real self, the true nature, the radiant personality. And the beauty that he sees will fill him with a passionate yearning, both to give and to possess. He will want both to give the utmost and best of himself, and also to possess what so satisfies all the cravings of the soul. And whether it be to give or to possess that he most wants he will be unable to distinguish. But, in the craving to give and possess, the highest stimulus will be afforded him to exert every faculty to its limit. The effort will give zest, and with zest will come added powers of vision, so that he will be able to see both her and his inmost and utmost capabilities. And though the force of outward circumstances may prevent both her and him from ever completely fulfilling those latent possibilities, what they see of themselves and of each other in those divine moments may nevertheless be a perfectly true vision of their real and fundamental nature. Love is not so blind as is supposed. Love is capable of seeing clearer and deeper than any other faculty.

What the Artist now sees with the eyes of Love will be the ground upon which he will have to form his judgment in the most critical decision of his life. For the moment will now have come when he will have to decide whether of all others he will give himself to her, and whether he can presume to ask of her that she will give herself to him—and each to the other for all the rest of their lives. It is a momentous decision to have to make. With his highly developed power of vision he will have divined her true nature. But he will have now to exercise his judgment on it—whether it will satisfy the needs of his whole being and whether his whole being is sufficient to satisfy her needs. Each has to be sure that his peculiar nature satisfies—and satisfies fully—his or her own peculiar needs, and that his peculiar nature satisfies the other's needs. A wrong decision here is fatal. The responsibility is fearful. All will depend upon his keenness of vision, his capacity for discrimination, and his soundness of judgment. The decision may be arrived at swiftly and consciously, or it may be come to unconsciously, gradually, and imperceptibly. But shorter or longer the time, consciously or unconsciously the method, it will have in the end to be made in a perfectly definite fashion—yes or no—and from that decision there can be no going back. And on that clear decision will hang the future welfare not only of the one who makes it, but of both. Each, therefore, has to decide for the welfare of both.

This is the real Day of Judgment. And each is his own judge. Now all his and her past life and inborn nature is being put to the test in a fierce ordeal—and the fiery ordeal of love is more searching even than the ordeal of war. Every smallest blot and blemish, every slightest impurity is shown up in startling clearness. Every flaw at once betrays itself. What will not bear a strain immediately breaks down. There is not an imperfection which is not glaringly displayed. The other may not see it, but he himself will—and upon him is the responsibility.

No wonder that both the one and the other hesitate to commit themselves finally and irrevocably! Can he with all his blots and blemishes, his failings and weaknesses, offer to give himself to the other? Is he worthy to receive all that he would expect to receive in return? Is he justified in asking that the whole being and the most sacred thing in life should be given over utterly to him? It seems astounding that any man should ever have the impudence to answer such questions in the affirmative. Doubtless he would not have had such effrontery but for two considerations.

In the first place he knows that, imperfect as he may be—downright sinful as he may often have been—he is not bad at bottom. At heart, he knows for certain he has capacities for improvement which would come at once into being if only they had the opportunity for development. And he knows that the other could make those opportunities—could provide the stimulus which would awaken in him and bring to fruit many a hidden capability of good. Every faculty in him he now feels being quickened to an activity never known before. Blemishes he feels being purged away in the cleansing fires of pure love. He feels that with the other he will be, as he has never been before, his whole and his true self. And this is the first consideration which gives him confidence.

The second is that he feels himself now to a very special degree in direct and intimate touch with the central Heart of Nature. Something from what he feels by instinct is the Divine Source of Life and Love comes springing up within him, penetrating him through and through, supporting and upholding him and urging him forward. He feels that he directly springs from that Source, and that it will ever sustain him as long as he is true to his own real self, and works for those high ends towards which he feels himself impelled.

With strong faith, then, he makes his decision—with strong faith in *himself,* for he knows himself to be inspired by the same great Spirit which animates the whole world of which he is himself a part. And having in this faith made his decision, he girds himself for the poignant battle of love.

And as in war so in love men—and women—rise to altogether unexpected heights of courage, endurance, and devotion. War is a fine spur to excellence. But love is an even finer. Every faculty is quickened and refined. Every high quality brought into fullest exercise. Daring and caution, utter disregard of self and selfishness in the extreme, are alike required. For the two will never achieve full wedded union until they have fought their way through many an interposing obstacle. Adroitness, and that rare quality, social courage, will be needed in dealing with ever-recurring, complicated, painful, and nerve-straining situations. Even in their attitude towards one another as they gradually come together the finest address will be required. For each has necessarily to be comparing himself and comparing the object of his love with others; and each feels that he is being similarly compared. There can be no final assurance till the union is completed. A single ill-judged word or action may ruin all. At any moment another may be preferred—or at least one of the two may find the other inadequate or deficient.

All this will afford the highest stimulus to emulation. Each will strive to excel in what the other approves and appreciates—or at any rate to excel in what is his own particular line. He will be incited to show himself at his best and to be his best.

But before the bliss of completest union is attained anguish and rapture in exquisite extremes will be experienced. For the soul of each will be exposed in all its quivering sensitiveness, and any but the most delicate touch will be a torture to it. Fortitude of the firmest will be required to bear the wounds which must necessarily come from this exposure. Each, too, will have to bear the pain of the suffering they must inevitably be causing to some few others—and those others among their very dearest.

As the intimacy of union becomes closer and closer the call for bodily union will become more and more insistent. In the first instance—and this is a point which is specially worth noting—the desire was *entirely* for spiritual union, for union of the *spirits* of each. What each admired and loved in the other was his or her capacity for love. He realised what a wonderful love the other *could* give. And he yearned with all his heart to have that love directed towards himself. It was a purely spiritual union that his heart was set on. The thought of bodily union did not enter his head. But the need for bodily touch as a means of expressing human feeling is inherent in human nature, and becomes more and more urgent as the feeling becomes warmer. Friends have to shake hands with each other and pat each other on the back in order to show the warmth of their feeling for one another. Women affectionately embrace one another. Parents and children, brothers and sisters, kiss one another. It is impossible adequately to express affection without bodily touch. And in the case of lovers, as the love deepens so also deepens the compelling need to express this love in bodily union of the closest possible.

And so the supreme moment arrives when each gives himself wholly, utterly, and for ever to the other—body, soul, and spirit—and they twain are one. And the remarkable result ensues that each in giving himself to the other has become more completely and truly himself than he has ever been before. He strives to become more and more closely wedded with the other. He yearns to give himself more completely and longs that there was more of himself to give. And he gives himself as completely as he can. Yet he has never before been so fully himself. The closeness and intimacy of the union, and all that he has received, has enabled him to bring forth and give utterance to what had lain deep and dormant within him—all his fondest hopes, his dearest dreams, his highest aspirations. Each is more himself in the other. He is, indeed, not himself without the other. Each has won possession of the other. Each has with joy and gladness given himself to the other. Each belongs to the other. Each is all the world to the other—a treasure without price. He is ever after in her as her own being. And she is in him as his own being. Apart from each other they are never again themselves. They are absorbed in mutual joy in one another.

The intensity of delight is more than they can bear. It brims up and overflows and goes bursting out to all the world. By being able to be their whole selves they have become more closely in touch with the deepest Heart of Nature and nearest the Divine. In that hushed and sacred moment when the ecstasy of life and love is at its highest they have never felt stronger, purer, lighter, nearer the Divine. They have reached deep down to the most elemental part of their nature. And they have soared up highest to the most Divine. But Divine and elemental, spiritual and bodily, seem one. There seems to be nothing bodily which is not spiritual. And nothing elemental which is not Divine.

It is not often that they will attain these culminating heights of spiritual exaltation. Nor will they be able long to remain there. The lark, the eagle, the airman, have all to come to earth again. And they spend most of their lives on the earth. But the lovers will have known what it is to soar. They will have found their wings. They will have seen heaven once, and breathed its air. And all nature, all human relationships, will be for ever after transfigured in heaven's light.

The state of being to which these twain have now arrived is the highest and best in life. This spiritual union of man and woman—this union of their souls which their bodily union has made possible in completeness—is that which of all else has most value. The friendship of men for men and women for women is high up in the scale of being. But it is not at the supreme summit. The holy union of man and woman is higher still, because it is a relation of the *whole* being of each to the other, and because it brings both into direct and closest contact with the Primal Source of Things, and on the line which points them highest. The relationship satisfies the *whole* needs of the selves of each and satisfies the urgency of the Heart of Nature.

* * *

So now our Artist will have experienced true spirituality in its highest degree; and having experienced also the most elemental in his nature, he will perforce have come in touch with Nature along her whole range. And his soul being at the finest pitch of sensitiveness, he will be able to appreciate Natural Beauty as never before. And nothing less than *natural* beauties, and nothing less than these beauties at their best, will in his exalted mood be satisfying to him. He will be driven irresistibly into the open air and the warm sunshine, and to the bosom of Mother-Earth. And there in the blue of heaven and in dreamy clouds; in the wide sea, or in tranquil lakes; in ethereal mountains or in verdant woodlands; in the loveliness of flowers, and in the music of the birds, he will find that which his spirit seeks—that to which his spirit wants to give response. Only there in the open, in the midst of Nature, will he find horizons wide enough, heights high enough, beauties rich enough, for his soul's needs.

The flowers as he looks into them will disclose glories of colour, texture, form, and fragrance he never yet had seen. The comely forms of trees, their varying greenery, and the dancing sunlight on the leaves, will fill him with an intensity of delight that heretofore he had never known. And as once more he goes among his fellow-men he will see them in a newer and a truer light. His contact with them will be easier; his friendships deeper; his certainty of affection surer; and his capacity for entering into every joy and sorrow immeasurably enlarged.

Through his love, our ideal Artist will have been enabled to reach deeper into the Heart of Nature than he had ever reached before, and to feel more intimately at one with her. And being thus in warmest touch with her, Natural Beauty, strong, deep, and delicate as only finest love can disclose, will be revealed to him. Enjoyment of Natural Beauty in its perfection is the prize he will have won.

CHAPTER X.
THE NATURE OF NATURE

The Artist is now in a position to take stock of Nature as a whole, of her nature, methods, and manner of working, of the motives which actuate her—of what, in short, she really is at heart. And having thus reviewed her, he will have to determine whether his wider and deeper knowledge of Nature confirms or detracts from the impression of her which he had gained from a contemplation of the forest's innumerable life. Upon this decision will depend his final attitude towards her. And upon his attitude towards her depends his capacity for enjoying Natural Beauty. For if he has any doubt in his mind as to the goodness of Nature or any hesitation about giving himself out to her, there is little prospect of his seeing Beauty in her. He will remain cold and unresponsive to her calls and enjoyment of Natural Beauty will not be for him.

And each of us—each for himself—just as much as the Artist will have to make up his mind on this fundamental question. If we are to get the full enjoyment we should expect out of Natural Beauty we must have a clear and firm conception in our minds of what Nature really is, what is her essential character, whether at heart she is cold and callous or warm and loving. So far as we were justified in drawing conclusions regarding the character of Nature as a whole from what we saw of her manifestations in the life of the forest, we came to the conclusion that she was not so hard and repellent as she assuredly would be to us if her guiding principle of action were the survival of the fittest. We inferred, rather, from our observations of her in the forest that she was actuated by an aspiration towards what we ourselves hold to be of most worth and value. We were therefore not disillusioned by closer familiarity with her, but more closely drawn towards her, and therefore prepared to see more Beauty in her. Now we have to review Nature as a whole—that is, in the Starry World as well as on this Earth—and see if the same conclusions hold good, and if we are therefore justified in loving Nature, or if we should view her with suspicion and distrust, hold ourselves aloof from her, and cultivate a stoic courage in face of a Power whose character we must cordially dislike.

There are men who hold that the appearance of life and love on this Earth is a mere flash in the pan and comes about by pure chance. They believe that life will be extinguished in a twinkling as we collide with some other star, or will simply flicker out again as the Sun's heat dies down and the Earth becomes cold. If this view be correct, then that impression of the reliability and kindliness of Nature which we formed when contemplating the stars in the desert would be a false impression; our feelings of friendship with Nature would at once freeze up and our vision of Beauty vanish like a wraith.

Fortunately Truth and Knowledge do not deal so cruel a blow at Beauty. Far from it: they take her side. There are no grounds for supposing that either chance or mechanism produces spirit, or that from merely physical and chemical combinations spirit can emerge. Spirit is no casual by-product of mechanical or chemical processes. Spirit is the governing factor regulating and controlling the physical movements—controlling them, indeed, with such orderliness that we may be apt from this very orderliness to regard the whole as a machine and fail to see that all is directed towards high spiritual ends.

If we are to appeal to reason, it is much more reasonable to assume that spirit always existed, and that the conditions for the emergence of life were brought about on purpose, than to assume that spirit is a mere excretion, like perspiration, of chemical processes. Certainly the former assumptions more clearly fit the facts of the case. For these facts are, firstly, that we spiritual selves exist, next that we have ideas of goodness and a determination to achieve it, next that plant as well as animal life on this Earth is purposive, then that the stars, numbering anything from a hundred to a thousand million, each of them a sun and many of them presumably with planets, are made of the same materials as this Earth, the plants, animals, and ourselves are composed of; that these materials have the same properties; that the same fundamental laws of gravitation, heat, motion, chemical and electrical action prevail there as here; and lastly that they are all connected with the Earth by some medium or continuum of energies, which enables vibrations, of which the most obvious are the vibrations of light, to reach the Earth from them. These facts point towards the conclusion that the whole Universe, as well as ourselves and the animals and plants on this Earth, is actuated by spirit. Goodness we have seen to be working itself out on the Earth; and there is nothing we see in the world of stars that prevents us from concluding that in the Universe as well as on the Earth what *should* be is the ground of what *is*.

Something higher than life, or life in some higher form than we know, may indeed have been brought into being among the stars. Life has appeared in an extraordinary variety of forms on this Earth, and it would necessarily appear in other forms elsewhere. And it is not difficult to imagine more perfect forms in which it might have developed. We men are the most highly developed beings on this planet. But our eyes and ears and other organs of sense take cognisance of only a few of the vibrations raining in upon our bodies from the outside world. There is a vast range of vibrations of the medium in which we are immersed of which our bodily organs take no cognisance whatever. If we had better developed organs we would be in much more intimate touch with the world about us, and be aware of influences and existences we are blind to now. Beings with these superior faculties may very possibly have come into existence among the stars.

Nor is there anything unreasonable in the assumption that from the inhabitants of these stars in their *ensemble* issue influences which directly affect conditions on this Earth; that in the all in its togetherness is Purpose; and that it was due to the working of this Purpose that conditions were produced on the Earth which made the emergence of life possible. To some it may seem that it was only by chance that the atoms and molecules happened to come together in such a particular way that from the combination the emergence of life was possible. To men of such restricted vision it would seem equally a matter of chance that a heavenly song resulted when a dozen choirboys came together, opened their mouths and made a noise. But men of wider vision would have seen that this song was no matter of chance, but was the result of the working out of a purpose; that the choirboys were brought together for a purpose; and that that purpose was resident in each of a large number of people scattered about a parish, but who, though scattered, were all animated by the same purpose of maintaining a choir to sing hymns. So it is not unreasonable to suppose that when the particles came together under conditions that life resulted, they had been brought together in those conditions to fulfil a purpose resident in each of a number of beings and groups of beings scattered about the Universe, but who, though scattered, were nevertheless animated by the same purpose. Anyhow, this seems a more reasonable assumption than the assumption that the particles came together by pure chance.

Beings with these superior faculties may very possibly have emerged among the stars. It would seem not at all improbable, therefore, that in some unrecognised way conditions on this Earth may be influenced in their general outlines by what is taking place in the Universe at large, in the same way as conditions in a village in India are affected by public opinion in England as epitomised in the decisions of the Cabinet. The remote Indian village is unaware that men in England have decided to grant responsible government to India in due course. And even if the villagers were told of this they would not realise the significance of the decision and how it would affect the fortunes of their village for good or ill during the next century or two. Conditions on this Earth may be similarly being affected by decisions made in other parts of the Universe—decisions the significance of which we would be as totally unable to recognise as the Indian villagers are to recognise the significance of the steps towards self-government which have just been made.

The Universe is so interconnected, and there is so much interaction between the parts and the whole, that the Earth may be more affected than we think by what goes on in the Universe at large. If there are higher levels of being among the stars, it may well be that the successive rises to higher levels on this Earth—from inorganic to organic, from organic to mental, and from the mental to the spiritual—have come about through this interaction between the parts and the whole. Conditions on this Earth may be more affected than we are aware of by the Universe in its ensemble, and by the actions of higher beings in other Earths.

In this very matter of Beauty, for example, it may quite possibly be the case that our intimation of Beauty has been received through the influence upon the most sensitive among us of beings in other parts of the Universe. We may be as unaware of the existence of those beings or of their having feelings towards us as the Indian villager is of the existence of the Cabinet in London or of the Cabinet's feelings towards him. But these stellar beings may be exerting their influence all the same. And it may be because of this influence that we men are able to see Beauty which escapes the eye of the eagle. Because of our higher receptiveness and responsiveness we may be able to receive and respond to spiritual calls from the Heart of Nature. And thus it may have been that we men learned to see Beauty, and now learn to see it more and more. There may be parts of the Universe where people live their lives in a blaze of Beauty, and are as anxious to impart to us their enjoyment of it as certain Freedom-loving Englishmen are to instil ideas of Freedom into the villagers of India.

These, at any rate, are among the possibilities of existence. It would be the veriest chance if on this little speck of an Earth the highest beings of all had come to birth. It may be so, of course. But the probabilities seem to be enormously great against it. It seems far more probable that among the myriads of stars some higher beings than ourselves have come into existence, and that conditions on this Earth are affected by the influence which they exert. We are under no compulsion whatever to believe that we men are completely at the mercy of blind forces or that chance rules supreme in Nature. We have firm ground for holding that it is spirit which is supreme, and that every smallest part and the whole together are animated by Purpose.

So when we view Nature in the tropical forests and in barren deserts, in mountains and in plains, in meadows and in woodlands, in seas and in stars, in animals and in men, we do not see Nature as a confused jumble with all her innumerable parts come together in haphazard fashion as the grains of sand shovelled into a heap—a chance aggregate of unrelated particles in which it is a mere toss-up which is next to which and how they are arranged. Nature is evidently not a chance collection of unrelated particles. We came to that conclusion when studying the forest, and a study of the stars shows nothing to weaken that conclusion. Nature is animated by Purpose.

Yet because Nature is animated by Purpose, we need not regard her as a machine, a piece of mechanism which has been designed and put together, wound up and set going by some outside mechanician, and regard ourselves as cogs on the wheels, watching all the other wheels go round and through the maze of machinery catching sight of the mechanician standing by and watching his handiwork. A cog on the wheel as it revolved would be rigidly confined in its operations: it would have no choice as to what means it should employ to carry out its end. Yet even plants have the power of choice, as we have seen, and use different means to achieve the same end. They also spend their entire lives in selecting and rejecting—in selecting and assimilating what will nourish their growth and enable them to propagate their kind, and in rejecting what would be useless or harmful. These are something more than mechanical operations; and if Nature were a machine, not even plants, much less animals and men, could have been produced. The operations of Nature, though orderly, are not mechanical only, and we cannot regard Nature as a machine.

And if Nature is purposive, she is at work at something more than the completion of a prearranged plan. We do not picture Nature as a *structure*, as a Cathedral, for example, designed by some super-architect, in process of construction. In a Cathedral each stone is perfectly and finally shaped and placed in a position in which it must ever after remain, and the whole shows signs of gradual completion as it is being built, and when it is built remains as it is. The architect has made I and carried out his plan, and there is an end of the matter. It is not thus that we view Nature, for everywhere we see signs of perfectibility in the component parts and in the whole together. Only if the Cathedral had in it the power to be continually making its foundations deeper, to be ever towering higher, and to be perpetually shaping itself into sublimer form, should we look on Nature as a Cathedral. But in that case the mind of the architect would have to dwell in each stone and in all together, and the Cathedral would be something more than a structure in the ordinary use of the word.

Nature is not a chance collection of particles, nor is she a mere machine, nor some kind of structure like a Cathedral in course of construction. But she is a Power of some kind, and what we have to determine is the kind of Power she is. Now we have seen that running through the life of the forest, controlling and directing the whole, is an Organising Activity. And our observation of the stars leads us to think that this same Organising Activity runs through them also. There is quite evidently an Activity at work keeping the whole together—the particles which go to form great suns, the particles which go to form a flower, and the particles which go to form a man; and all in their togetherness. Only we would not look upon this Activity as working anywhere outside Nature: we would look for it within her. We would not regard it as emanating from some kind of spiritual central sun situated among the stars midway between us and the farthest star we see—as irradiating from some sort of centrally-situated spiritual power-house. As we look up into the starry heavens we cannot imagine the Activity as residing in the empty space between the stars or between the stars and the Earth on which we stand. It seems absurd to picture its dwelling-place there. Equally absurd does it seem to regard the Activity as emanating from some spiritual sun situated far beyond the confines of the stars, and from there emitting spiritual rays upon Nature, including us men. As we look out upon Nature we see that the Activity which animates her does not issue from any outside source, but is actually in her.

We do not need to look for the seat of that animating Activity in the empty spaces of the starry heavens or anywhere beyond them. We look for it in the stars themselves, in our own star, in the Earth, in every particle of which the stars and Sun and Earth are composed, in every plant and animal, and in every human heart, and in the whole together. There it is—and especially in the human heart—that the soul of Nature resides. There is its dwelling-place. To each of us it is nearer than father is to son. It is as near as "I" am to each one of the myriad particles which in their togetherness go to make up the body and soul which is "me." The spirit of Nature is resident in no remoteness of cold and empty space. It is deep within us and all around us. It permeates everything and everybody, everywhere and always. And if we wish to be unmistakably aware of its presence, we have only to look within ourselves, and whenever we are conscious of a higher perfection which something within, responding to the influences impinging insistently on us, is urging us to achieve; whenever we have a vision of something more perfect, more lovely, more lovable, and feel ourselves urged on to reach after that greater perfection—we are in those moments directly and unmistakably experiencing the Divine Spirit of Nature. Whenever we feel the Spirit within us showing us greater perfectibility and prompting us to make ourselves and others more perfect than we have been we are, in that moment, being directly influenced by the Spirit of Nature itself. We are receiving inspiration direct from the genius of Nature, the *driving* Spirit which is continually urging her on, and the *directing* Spirit which guides her to an end. We are in touch with the true Heart of Nature.

So as we take a comprehensive view of Nature both in her outward bodily form and her inner spiritual reality, and find her to be an interconnected whole in which all the parts are interrelated with one another, one body and one mind, self-contained and self-conscious, and driven by a self-organising, self-governing, self-directing Activity—we should regard her as nothing *less* than a *Personal Being.* In ordinary language we speak of Nature as a Person, and when we so speak we should not regard ourselves as speaking figuratively: we should mean quite literally and as a fact that she is a Person. And we should look upon that Personal Being, in which we are ourselves included, as in process of realising an ideal hidden within her—an ideal which in its turn is ever perfecting itself.

* * *

What is meant by Nature being a Person, and a Person actuated by a hidden ideal, and being in process of realising that ideal, and what is meant by an ideal perfecting itself, may be best explained with the help of an illustration.

First it will be necessary to explain how we can regard Nature as a *Person,* or at least as nothing less than a Person—though possibly *more.* It is contended by many authorities that we cannot regard any collective being, such as a college or a regiment—and Nature is a collective being— as a true person. But their arguments are unconvincing. They allow that "I" am a person because "I" possess rationality and self-consciousness. But "I" am a system or organisation of innumerable beings—electrons, groupings of electrons, groups of groupings in rising complexity. "I"—the body and soul which makes up "me"—am nothing but a collective being myself. And if we take the case of "England" as an example of a collective being, we shall see that England has as much right to be considered a personal being as any single Englishman, composed as he is of innumerable separate beings.

Perhaps to one who is representing England among strange peoples the personality of England is more apparent than to those who are constantly living in England itself. To the foreign people among whom this representative is living England is a very real person. What she thinks about them, what she does, what her intentions are, what is her character and disposition, are matters of high interest; for upon England's good or ill will towards them may perhaps depend to a large extent their own future. Viewed from a distance like that, England quite obviously does possess a *character* of her own. She appears to some people large-hearted and generous; to others aggressive and domineering; to most solid, sensible, reasonable, steadfast, and steady. And to all she has a character quite distinctive and her own—quite different from the character of France or of Russia. And England with equal obviousness *thinks*. She forms her own opinions of other nations, of their character, intentions, activities, and feelings. She thinks over her own line of action in regard to them. She takes decisions. And she *acts*. She is for a long time suspicious of Russia, and takes measures to defend herself against any possible hostile Russian action. She later comes to the conclusion that there is no fundamental difference between her and Russia, so she takes steps to compose the superficial differences. Later still, when both she and Russia are being attacked by a common enemy, she deliberately places herself on terms of closest friendship with Russia, and both gives her help and receives help from her. At the same time, having come to the conclusion that Germany is threatening her very life, she makes war on Germany, and prosecutes that war with courage, endurance, steadfastness and intelligence, and with a determination to win at any cost. England has deep *feeling*, too. She had a feeling of high exaltation on the day she determined to fight for her life and freedom. She had a feeling of sadness and anxiety as things went against her at Mons, Ypres, Gallipoli, Kut. She was wild with joy when the war was victoriously concluded. And she was proud of herself as she thought how among the sister nations of the Empire of which she was the centre, and among the allied nations, she had played a great and noble part.

Now when a body, like England, can thus think for itself, form its own decisions, take action, establish friendships, fight enemies, and feel deeply, surely that body must possess personality. In ordinary language England is always spoken of as a person. And ordinary language speaks with perfect accuracy in this respect.

In her relations with individual Englishmen England also shows her personality. The representative abroad feels very vividly how she *expects* him to act in certain ways—ways in accordance with her character and her settled line of action. And she conveys these expectations to him not only in formal official instructions from her Government: the most important of those expectations are conveyed in a far more subtle and intimate but most unmistakable way. The English Government did not write officially to Nelson at Trafalgar that England expected every man to do his duty. But Nelson, standing there for England, knew very well that this was what England was expecting of him and of those serving under him. A representative would find it very hard to locate the exact dwelling-place of the heart and soul and mind of England, whether in Parliament, or in the Press, or in the Universities, or in factories, or in the villages. But that there is an England expecting him to behave himself in accordance with her traditions and character, and to act on certain general but quite definite lines, and who will admire and reward him if he acts faithfully to her expectations, and condemn and in extreme cases punish him if he is unfaithful, he has not the shadow of a doubt. Nor does he doubt that this England, besides expecting a certain general line of conduct, will and can *constrain* him to act in accordance with her settled determination—that she has authority and has power to give effect to her will.

And the official governmental representatives are not the only representatives of England. *Every* Englishman is a representative of England. How representative he is he will experience as he finds himself among strange peoples outside his own country. He will find then that he has certain traits and traditions and characteristics which clearly distinguish him from the people among whom he is travelling. And unofficial though he may be, he will yet feel England expecting him to behave as an Englishman. And though he may not be so vividly aware of it when he is at home, he is still a representative of England when he is in England itself. In everyday life he is being expected and constrained by England to act in certain ways.

Nor is it all a one-sided affair—England expecting so much of him and he having no say or control over what England does. On the contrary, the relationship is mutual. He goes to the making and shaping of England just as much as she goes to the making and shaping of him. He expects certain behaviour of her as she expects such of him. And if he has gained the confidence of his fellow-countrymen and has energy and determination, he may do much to affect her destiny.

England is therefore, so it seems, a *person* just as much as a single Englishman is a person. Englishmen, in fact, only attain their full personality in an England which *has* personality.

* * *

Now Nature, I suggest, in spite of what has been said against the view, is a Person in exactly the same way as England is a person. Nature is a collective being made up of component beings—self-active electrons, self-active atoms, self-active suns and planets, self-active cells, plants, animals, men, and groups and nations of men—as England is made up of the land of England and all that springs therefrom, including the Englishmen themselves. Nature thinks and feels and strives as England thinks and feels and strives. And Nature cares for her children as England looks after her sons. It is often said, indeed, that Nature is hard and cruel. But it is only through the unfailing regularity and reliability of her fundamental laws—of her "constitution"—that freedom and progress are possible. If we could not depend upon perfect law we could make no advance whatever. We should all be abroad and uncertain. Yet in spite of her unbending rigidity over fundamentals, she does also show mercy and pity. A child toddling along downhill unregardful of the force of gravitation falls on its face and screams with pain. But Nature, represented by the mother, rushes up, seizes the little thing in her arms, presses it lovingly to her bosom, rock it and coaxes it and covers it with kisses.

So if Nature can think and feel and strive and show mercy and loving-kindness, she is entitled to the dignity of personality. And when we stand back and regard Nature as a whole, we shall look upon her as a Person and nothing less.

* * *

We have now to understand what is meant by saying that Nature is a Person actuated by a hidden ideal and being in process of realising that ideal. When travelling across the Gobi Desert I found a yellow rose—a dwarf, simple, single rose. It is known to botanists as *Rosa persica,* and is believed to be the original of all roses. I found it on the extreme outlying spurs of the Altai Mountains. Now, a seed of the rose, partly under the influence of its surroundings (soil, moisture, air, sunshine) but chiefly *by virtue of something which it contains within itself,* something inherent in its very nature, will grow up into a rose-bush and give forth roses. The seed develops into a rose, not because some outside super-gardener takes hold of each one of the million million ultra-microscopic particles of which it is made up and puts it carefully into its appointed place, as a builder might put the stones of a building into their exact places according to the plans of an architect; but because each of those minutest ultimate particles has that within it which prompts it to act of its own accord in response to the call of the whole. Each of these electrons is in incessant and terrific motion, moving at the rate of something like 180,000 miles a second, so placing it in position would be a difficult matter. Besides which, each electron is not a tiny bit of matter as we ordinarily conceive matter—something which we can touch and handle. It is a mere centre or nucleus of energy. Any placing of it in position by a super-gardener is therefore out of the question. Each of those little particles moves and acts of itself in accordance with its own inner promptings, and in response to the influence of those other myriads of particles and groups of particles about it. And that system of these groups of particles which is enclosed within the rondure of the seed must have within it the ideal of the rose to be. Each particle will act on its own initiative, but all will act under the mutual influence of one another, and in their togetherness will make up the rose-spirit, being informed by the ideal of the rose which in its turn will suffuse the whole. And this rose-spirit—this rose-disposition—as it gives itself play, so controls and directs their movements that eventually the full-blown rose comes into being.

What happens is, we may imagine, much the same as what happened in the case of Australia. A handful of settlers from the mother-country formed the germ-seed from which the Australia of to-day has grown up. There was no external despot ordering each individual Australian to do this, that, and the other—to come this way and go that, and to stop in one place this year and in another place the next. Each Australian acting on his own initiative, and all in their togetherness, created the Australian spirit, which again reacting upon each Australian induced him to act in accordance with that spirit. And so in time Australia, assimilating individuals from outside and absorbing them into its texture, and imbuing them with the Australian spirit, grew up into manhood in the Great War and astonished the world by its strong individuality, its character, intelligence, determination, and good comradeship.

In the same way these particles of the rose-seed, each acting of itself, in their collectivity formed the rose-spirit. And each was in turn imbued by the rose-spirit. They had in them unconsciously the ideal of the rose-bush with its roots, stem, branches, leaves, flowers, fruit, seed. In all their activities they were actuated by this ideal. It was always constraining them in the given direction. By reason of the working of it in the particles they could by no possibility arrange themselves into a may tree or a lilac bush. There was an inner core of activity which persisted through all the countless changes of the process, which permeated the whole and which kept it directed to the particular end it had all the time in view. That activity had, in fact, a well-defined disposition, and that disposition was defined by the ideal of the rose, and was to form a rose-bush bearing roses.

That the rose-seed developed into the rose was due, therefore, not to the operation of any outside agent, but was due to the operation of the rose-spirit that it had within it, and which was persistently driving it to bring into actual being that ideal of the rose which was the essence of its spirit. The ideal of the rose was the motive-power of the whole process.

Where the rose-spirit derived from we shall later on enquire. Here we must note a point of the utmost importance. The seed of this *Rosa persica* is imbued with the spirit of *Rosa persica*. It has this ideal working within it. But it is not confined within the rigid limits of that ideal. It has that ideal, but *something beyond also*—something in the *direction* of that ideal, but stretching on ahead to an illimitable distance. The rose-seed developed riot only into the rose-flower, but through the flowers into numerous rose-seeds. And from the original *Rosa persica* seeds have sprung roses of scores of varieties. Roses of every variety of form, colour, habit, texture are constantly appearing. By purposeful mating, and supplying favourable conditions of soil, temperature, etc., almost any kind of variety can be produced. So we have not only yellow roses of every shade from gold and cream to lemon, but also white and red and pink roses of every hue. We have single roses and roses as full as small cabbages. And we have dwarf roses and roses climbing 50 or 60 feet in height.

From all this it is evident that within the original seed of *Rosa persica* was a rose-spirit which refused to be confined within the limits of *Rosa persica* only, but stretched out far beyond as well. The rose-spirit had latent in it, and was unconsciously stretching out to, all the beauties which roses have since attained to, and beyond that again to all the beauties that are yet to come. The horizon of the rose-spirit was never confined by a single plan—the plan of the *Rosa persica*—as the builder is confined by the plan of the architect, beyond which he cannot go. The rose-spirit could reach out along the line of roses to an unlimited extent. It could produce nothing but roses; it could not produce laburnums. But it could produce roses of unlimited variety, provided favourable conditions were available.

But the *Rosa persica* was itself the outcome of a long line of development from a far-away primordial plant-germ. From that original plant-germ have sprung all the ferns and grasses, the shrubs and trees and flowers, of the present day. So in that plant-germ must have resided the plant-spirit with an ideal of all this variety of plant-life actuating it—unconsciously, of course, but most effectively for all that. The particles of that original germ in their individual activities and in their mutual influence upon one another were in their togetherness actuated by a plant-spirit which had in mind—so to speak—not only the reproduction of a plant precisely similar to the original plant, but one with the possibilities of development and of reproducing others with possibilities of still further development. All that plant life has so far attained and all that it will attain to in future—perhaps also all that it *might* have attained to—must have been present in the plant-spirit of that original plant-germ. And it is through the working out—the realising—of this ideal which actuated that plant-spirit, and through the response which this spirit made to the stimulus of its surroundings that all the wonderful development of plant life has taken place. The plant-spirit had to keep within the lines of plant life; it could not stray beyond it to develop lions and tigers. But within the lines of plant life it could stretch out to illimitable distances. All that was wanted was the stimulus of favourable conditions, and from its surroundings it could select, reject, assimilate, all that would further its end.

* * *

In the Gobi Desert I also saw the wild horse—*Equus Prjevalskyi*—supposed to be the original horse. And as the rose springs from the seed, so the horse develops from the ovum. And by virtue of the horse-spirit, the horse-ideal, by which all the innumerable particles of that ovum is actuated, it develops into a horse, and not into a donkey or a cow. But the ovum of the original *Equus Prjevalskyi* must have had in it the ideal of something more than the *Equus Prjevalskyi*, for from the original stock has sprung the great variety of horses we see to-day—race-horses, cart-horses, hunters, polo ponies, Shetland ponies, etc. And these are still varying. And the *Equus Prjevalskyi* was itself the outcome of a long line of development. Like all other animals, including man, it must have sprung from an original animal-germ. And the particles of that original animal-germ must have had in them the animal-spirit actuated by the ideal of all the animals of the present day, including man, and ready to develop as soon as favourable conditions provided the necessary stimulus to which the germ was ready to respond.

And both the original plant-germ and the original animal-germ sprang from an original plant-animal germ. And this, again, from the Earth itself. So that the Earth must always have had hidden in it the ideal of all plant and animal and human life—and not only the ideal of what it has reached at present, but of all it *will* become, and, it is important to note, of all it *might* become in future. It is the working of this ideal in the Earth, from the time five hundred million years or so ago when it budded off from the Sun as a fiery mist, that it has, under the influence of the light and heat of the Sun, and possibly also under the influences from the Stellar Universe as well, produced what we see to-day. The Earth-Spirit was inspired by this ideal, and in the ideal was this capacity for improving itself. And through the working of this ideal, and under the influence of the rest of the world, the Earth has developed from a flaming sphere into a molten ball, into a globe of barren land and sea, and so on into the verdure-covered and animal- and man-inhabited Earth of the present age. The Earth, like the rose-seed, contained within it a core of Activity which permeated every particle and constrained it with its fellow-particles to direct itself towards the ideal—a core of Activity which was animated by the ideal, while the ideal on its part had an innate faculty of perfecting itself.

But the Earth is itself only a minute mite even of the Solar System. And the Sun is only one of perhaps a thousand million other stars, some so distant that light travelling at the rate of 186,000 miles a second must have started from them before the birth of Christ to reach us to-day. Nevertheless the Earth is composed of the same ultimate particles of matter that even the most distant stars are made of. The Earth, the Sun and stars, are composed of electrons which are all alike. Doubtless there are individual differences between electrons as there are between men, but in a general way they are as much alike as all men appear alike to an eagle. And of these electrons the whole Universe is made as well as the Earth. The same laws of motion, of gravitation, and of electro-magnetic and chemical attraction, obtain there as here. The scale of the Stellar World is immensely larger than the scale we are accustomed to on this Earth. But the same fundamental laws everywhere prevail, and the Earth and stars are composed of the same material.

So it must have been from the Heart of Nature as a whole that the Earth-Spirit must have derived the ideal which actuated it. Deep in the Heart of Nature must have resided the ideal of the state of the Earth as it is to-day. In the great world as a whole, as in the rose-seed, must have been operating an ideal at least of what is on the Earth to-day, and of what this Earth will become and of what it might become; and possibly *also* of greater things which have already been realised, or *will* be realised and *might* be realised in the planets of other suns than our Sun. There must ever have been working throughout the Universe an Activity constraining the ultimate particles in a given direction. There must have been an Organising Activity, collecting the diffused particles together, grouping them into concentrated organisms and achieving loftier and loftier modes of being. Each of those inconceivably numerous and incredibly minute particles which make up the stars and the Earth and all on it—each one acted of itself. But each acted of itself under the influence of its fellows—that is, of every other particle; that is, of the *whole*. Each acted in response to its surroundings, but its surroundings were nothing short of the whole of Nature outside itself. Together they formed the Spirit of Nature with the ideal as its essence. And Nature in her turn acted on the particles— as Englishmen form the spirit of England and the spirit of England acts back upon individual Englishmen.

It was the working of this Spirit, with its self-improving ideal, that has produced Nature as we see her to-day. The distant ideal furnished the motive-power by which the whole is driven forward. And this ideal was itself built up by the unceasing interaction of the whole upon the parts and the parts upon the whole. What was in the parts responded to the stimulus of what was in the whole, and the whole was affected by the activity of the parts. What was immanent responded to what was transcendent. And the transcendence was affected by the immanence.

CHAPTER XI.
NATURE'S IDEAL

If we have been right so far, we have arrived at the position that Nature is a Personal Being in process of realising an ideal operating within herself. We have now to satisfy ourselves as to the character of that ideal. What is the full ideal working in the whole of Nature we cannot possibly know. We can only know so much of it as can be detected with our imperfect faculties on this minute atom of the Universe on which we dwell. We cannot be sure we have even discerned the highest levels of the ideal. For there may be higher beings than ourselves on the planets of the stars, and among those higher beings higher qualities than any we know of, or can conceive, may have emerged. Love is the highest quality we know. But love in any true sense of the word — love as a self-conscious activity — has only emerged with man, and man has only appeared within the last half-million of the Earth's four or five hundred million years of existence as the Earth. We cannot, therefore, presume to say what is the ideal in its highest development for the whole of Nature.

But from our experience here we can see what that ideal is up to (what for us is) a very high level, and we can make out what is apparently its fundamental characteristic. I obtained my best conception of it on the evening I left Lhasa at the conclusion of my Mission to Tibet in 1904, when I had an experience of such value for determining Nature's ideal, and, for me at any rate, so convincingly corroborative of the conclusions which others who have had similar experiences have drawn from them as to Nature's ideal, that I hope I may be excused for relating in some detail the circumstances in which it came to me.

These circumstances, though not the experience itself, were somewhat exceptional. I was at that particular moment at the highest pitch of existence — that is to say, of my own existence. I had had an unusually wide experience of the wild countries of that most interesting and varied of the continents — Asia, and for that reason had been specially selected for the charge of a Mission to Tibet. However ill-qualified I might be for other tasks, for this particular business of establishing neighbourly relations with a very secluded and seclusive Asiatic people, difficult of approach both on account of their natural disposition and of the mighty mountain barrier which stood between them and the rest of the world, I was esteemed to have peculiar qualifications. My comrades were also men selected for their special qualifications—one for his knowledge of the Tibetans, another for his knowledge of the Chinese, another for his knowledge of geology, and so on. The troops engaged were selected for their experience in frontier warfare, and each man had had to pass a medical test. We were at the top of our physical fitness and ripe in experience.

Besides British officers and a few British troops, there were among the soldiers Sikhs, Pathans, Gurkhas, a few Bengalis, a few Rajputs and Dogras; and among the followers were Bhutias and Lepchas from Sikkim, Baltis from Kashmir, Bhutanese from Bhutan. There were thus Christians, Mohammedans, Hindus, and Buddhists: men from an island in the Atlantic, and men from the remotest valleys of the Himalaya. And our destination had been a sacred city hidden two hundred miles behind the loftiest range of mountains in the world.

On our way we had had to battle with the elements of Nature in very nearly their extremest forms and in every variety. We started in the sweltering heat of the plains of India in the hottest season. We passed the lower outer ranges of the Himalaya in the midst of torrential rain, like the heaviest thunder-shower in England, continuing all day long and day after day with scarcely a break, and penetrating through a waterproof coat as if it were paper. Following this we had to cross the main axis of the Himalaya in January, to pass the winter at an altitude of 15,000 feet above sea-level, and face blizzards which cut through heavy fur coats and left us as if we were standing before it in our bare bones.

We had also had to battle with the Tibetans—not only in actual fighting, but in diplomacy as well. I had deliberately risked my life in order to effect a settlement by persuasion and without resort to arms. Officers and men at my request had done the same. Subsequently we had both attacked and been attacked. Five hundred of us had for two months to face the attacks of eight thousand Tibetans. Later, again, we had had a long, tough, diplomatic contest with the Tibetans.

Besides battling with the elements and with the Tibetans, I had also had to battle with my own people—as is always and inevitably the case on such occasions. Military and political considerations had to contend against each other. This local question between India and Tibet was part of the general international question of the relations of European nations, Russia, France, Germany, Italy, America, with China, for Tibet was under the suzerainty of China. Local considerations had therefore to contend with international considerations. Then from the local point of view the permanent settlement of this particular question was desirable, whereas those responsible for the international situation would not object to a temporary arrangement of this single question as long as the whole general situation could be favourably secured. The Tibetan question was part of the whole question of our relations with Russia. Our relations with Russia were connected with our relations with France. We were coming to an arrangement with France as regards Egypt and Morocco. If we did anything in Tibet which vexed Russia she might be troublesome as regards Egypt, and make it difficult to come to an arrangement with France and to bring off the Anglo-French Entente. Of all these international considerations I was kept aware by Government even in the heart of Tibet. But my position required that I should stand up for the political as against the military, the local as against the international, and the permanent settlement as against the temporary arrangement. It was my duty vigorously to battle for this—as it was equally the duty of the military and those responsible for international affairs to battle for their own point of view. And of course I had to submit, after contesting my standpoint, to the decision of those in authority; though I had to contend for the particular, it was the general which had to prevail.

In the end a settlement was reached, and in this remote city we had received congratulations from many different people in many different lands. The troops, my staff, and all about me were filled with delight at the success of our enterprise. Even the Tibetans themselves seemed pleased at the settlement; at any rate, they asked to be taken under our protection. On the morning we left Lhasa the Lama Regent, who in the absence of the Dalai Lama had conducted negotiations with us, paid us a farewell visit and gave us the impression of genuine goodwill towards us. We and the Tibetans had contended strongly against one another. But it seemed that a way had been found by which good relations between us could be maintained. We had discovered that fundamentally we were perfectly well-disposed towards each other, and means had been found for composing our differences. Throughout the Mission we had kept before us the supreme importance of securing this goodwill eventually. The Tibetan frontier runs with the Indian frontier for a thousand miles, and it would have been the height of folly to have stirred up in the Tibetans a lasting animosity. Far more important, then, than securing the actual treaty we regarded securing the permanent goodwill; and when I felt that through the exertion of my Staff and the good behaviour of the troops as well as through my own efforts the goodwill of the Tibetans really had been secured, my satisfaction was profound.

It was after enduring all these hardships, after running all these risks, and after battling in all these controversies, that this deep satisfaction came upon me. For though at times I felt, as every leader feels in like circumstances, that success must have been due to everyone else besides myself—to the backing and firm direction I had received from Government, to the sound advice and help of my Staff, to the bravery and endurance of the troops, without all or any one of which aids success would have been unattainable—yet I could not help also feeling that I had often on my own responsibility to make decisions and run risks, and to give advice to Government; and that if I had erred in my decisions or in the advice I gave or in taking the risks, success most assuredly would not have been achieved, however much support I received from elsewhere. I had, therefore, that satisfaction a man naturally feels when his special qualifications and training and the experience he has gained during the best part of his life have proved of acknowledged good to his country. And this was the frame of mind in which I rode out of Lhasa on our march homeward.

These were the circumstances in which I had the experience I now venture to describe. After arrival in camp I went off into the mountains alone. It was a heavenly evening. The sun was flooding the mountain slopes with slanting light. Calm and deep peace lay over the valley below me—the valley in which Lhasa lay. I seemed in tune with all the world and all the world seemed in tune with me. My experiences in many lands—in dear distant England; in India and China; in the forests of Manchuria, Kashmir, and Sikkim; in the desert of Gobi and the South African veldt; in the Himalaya mountains; and on many an ocean voyage; and experiences with such varied peoples as the Chinese and Boers, Tibetans and Mahrattas, Rajputs and Kirghiz—seemed all summed up in that moment. And yet here on the quiet mountain-side, filled as I was with the memories of many experiences that I had had in the high mountain solitudes and in the deserts of the world away from men, I seemed in touch with the wide Universe beyond this Earth as well.

After the high tension of the last fifteen months, I was free to let my soul relax. So I let it open itself out without restraint. And in its sensitive state it was receptive of the finest impressions and quickly responsive to every call. I seemed to be truly in harmony with the Heart of Nature. My vision seemed absolutely clear. I felt I was seeing deep into the true heart of things. With my soul's eye I seemed to see what was really in men's hearts, in the heart of mankind as a whole and in the Heart of Nature as a whole.

And my experience was this—and I try to describe it as accurately as I can. I had a curious sense of being literally in love with the world. There is no other way in which I can express what I then felt. I felt as if I could hardly contain myself for the love which was bursting within me. It seemed to me as if the world itself were nothing but love. We have all felt on some great occasion an ardent glow of patriotism. This was patriotism extended to the whole Universe. The country for which I was feeling this overwhelming intensity of love was the entire Universe. At the back and foundation of things I was certain was love—and not merely placid benevolence, but active, fervent, devoted love and nothing less. The whole world seemed in a blaze of love, and men's hearts were burning to be in touch with one another.

It was a remarkable experience I had on that evening. And it was not merely a passing roseate flush due to my being in high spirits, such as a man feels who has had a good breakfast or has heard that his investments have paid a big dividend. I am not sure that I was at the moment in what are usually called high spirits. What I felt was more of the nature of a deep inner soul-satisfaction. And what I saw amounted to this—that evil is the superficial, goodness the fundamental characteristic of the world; affection and not animosity the root disposition of men towards one another. Men are inherently good not inherently wicked, though they have an uphill fight of it to find scope and room for their goodness to declare itself, and though they are placed in hard conditions and want every help they can to bring their goodness out. Fundamentally men are consuming with affection for one another and only longing for opportunity to exert that affection. They want to behave straightly, honourably, and in a neighbourly fashion towards one another, and are only too thankful when means and conditions can be found which will let them indulge this inborn feeling of fellowship. Wickedness, of course, exists. But wickedness is not the essential characteristic of men. It is due to ignorance, immaturity, and neglect, like the naughtinesses of children. It springs from the conditions in which men find themselves, and not from any radical inclination within themselves. With maturity and reasonable conditions the innate goodness which is the essential characteristic will assert itself. This is what came to me with burning conviction. And it arose from no ephemeral sense of exhilaration, nor has it since evaporated away. It has remained with me for fifteen years, and so I suppose will last for the rest of my life. Of course in a sense there has been disillusionment, both as to myself and as to the world. As one comes into the dull round of everyday life the glow fades away and all seems grey and colourless. Nevertheless, the conviction remains that the glow was the *real,* and that the grey is the superficial. The glow was at the heart and is what some day *will* be—or, anyhow, *might* be.

An additional ground I have for believing it to be true is that on that mountain-side near Lhasa I had a specially favourable opportunity of looking at the world from, as it were, a proper focal distance. And it is only from a proper focal distance that we can see what things really are. If we put ourselves right up against a picture in the National Gallery we cannot possibly see its beauty—see what the picture really is. No man is a hero to his own valet. And that is not because a man is not a hero, but because the valet is too close to see the real man. Cecil Rhodes at close quarters was peevish, irritable, and like a big spoilt child. Now at a distance we know him, with all his faults, to have been a great-souled man. Social reformers near at hand are often intolerable bores and religious fanatics frequently a pestilential nuisance. We have to get well away from a man to see him as he really is. And so it is with mankind as a whole.

So I become more and more certain that my vision was true. And the experience of the Great War strengthens my conviction. As we recede from it, what will stand out, we may be sure, are not the crimes and cruelties that have been committed and the suffering that has been caused, but the astounding heroism which was displayed, the self-sacrifice, the devotion and love of country that were shown—heroism and devotion such as have never before in the world's history been approached, and which was manifested by common everyday men and women in every branch of life and in every country.

* * *

The conclusion I reach from this experience is that I was, at the moment I had it, intimately in touch with the true Heart of Nature. In my exceptionally receptive mood I was directly experiencing the genius of Nature in the very act of inspiring and vitalising the whole. I was seeing the Divinity in the Heart streaming like light and heat through every part of Nature, and with the dominating forcefulness of love lifting each to its own high level.

And my experience was no unique experience. It was an experience the like of which has come to many men and many women in every land in all ages. It may not be common; but it is not unusual. And in all cases it gives the same certainty of conviction that the Heart of Nature is *good*, that men are not the sport of chance, but that Divine Love is a real, an effectively determining and the dominant factor in the processes of Nature, and Divine fellowship the essence of the ideal which is working throughout Nature and compelling all things unto itself.

CHAPTER XII.
THE HEART OF NATURE

That Nature is a Personal Being—or at least nothing *less* than a Personal Being—that she is actuated by an ideal, and that her ideal, so far as we are able to judge, is an ideal of Divine Fellowship, is the conclusion at which we have now arrived. But we shall understand Nature better, and so see her Beauty more fully, if we can understand how she works out this ideal in detail. And we shall best understand how she works it out if we examine what goes on within our own selves and see how *we* work out the ideal with which we believe Nature herself has inspired us. For it is in ourselves that the dominating spirit of Nature is most clearly manifested to us. And being ourselves the instruments and agents of Nature, and informed through and through with her spirit, we ought to be able to understand how she works if only we look carefully enough into the working of our own inner selves.

What we find is that under the inspiration of the genius of Nature we are perpetually projecting in front of us a pattern or standard of what we think we ought to be, or should like to be, and of what we think our country and the world ought to be. We set up an ideal. It is generally very vague. But there is always at the back of our minds an idea of something more perfect. And this idea we bring out from time to time from its seclusion and set up before us as an end to aim at.

Sometimes we deliberately try to draw the outlines of this ideal more definitely. Each of us will picture a slightly different ideal to the rest. The ideal men will differ just as much as actual men, and the ideal countries as much as actual countries. No two will be exactly alike. And each of us will probably make his ideal man very different from himself—perhaps the exact opposite, for each will be peculiarly conscious of his own imperfections and shortcomings.

But if the ideal man which each sets up differs in small particulars from what others set up, the general outline of all will probably be very much the same, as men in general are much the same when compared with other animals. All will be based on the idea of fellowship. So aided by examples chosen from among our friends, we may here attempt to build up an ideal type of man. For the effort will help us to realise better both what Nature is aiming at and how she works.

Formerly we might have drawn this ideal man upright, straight, rigid, unbending. More recently we might have drawn him as a super-man, the fittest-to-survive kind of man, all muscular will, intent only on bending every other will to his and crashing relentlessly on through life like a bison in the forest. But nowadays we want a man with the same reliability as the upright type, but with grace and suppleness in place of rigidity; and with the same strength as the super-man, but with gentleness and consideration in proportion to the strength. We do not want a man of wood; and what we do want is not so much a super-man as a gentle-man—a man of courtesy and grace as well as strength.

The stiff and stilted type of a bygone age will have melted under the warmth of deepening fellowship and become flowing and fluid. The man of this type will not only be full of consideration for others, but will naturally, out of a full and overflowing heart and of his own generous prompting, eagerly enter into the lives and pursuits, the hopes and fears, the joys and sorrows of those with whom he is connected. And with all this wide *general* kindliness he will be something more than merely amiable and good-natured, and will have capacity for intense devotion for *particular* men and women. He will necessarily have fine tact and address, adroitness and skill in handling difficult and delicate situations, and the sensitiveness to appreciate the most hidden feelings of others. Wit and distinction he will have, too, with ability to discern the real nature of people and events, and to distinguish the best from the good, and the good from the indifferent and bad. He will also possess that peculiar sweetness of disposition which is only found when behind it is the surest strength. And with all his gentleness, tenderness, and capacity for sympathy he will have the grit and spirit to hold his own, to battle for his rights, and to fight for those conditions which are absolutely necessary for his full development. He will, in addition, have the initiative to think out and strike out his own line and to make his own mark.

He will be a man of the world in the sense of being accustomed to meet and mix with men in many different walks of life and of many different nationalities. And he will be a man of the home in the sense of being devoted to his own family circle. He will be at home in the town and at home in the country; adapted to the varied society, interests, and pursuits which town life can afford, but devoted also to the country, to the open air and elemental nature and animals and plants.

A fixed principle and firm determination with him will be to do his duty—to do his social duty, to do the right thing at whatever temporary cost to himself. The right thing for him will be that which produces most good. And he will deem that the most good which best promotes human fellowship, warms it with love, colours it with beauty, enlightens it with truth, and sweetens it with grace. Finally, and culminatingly, he will have that spirituality and fine sensitiveness of soul which will put him in touch with the true Heart of Nature and make him eagerly responsive to the subtlest promptings which spring therefrom; so he will be possessed of a profound conviction, rooted in the very depths of his being, that in doing the right thing, or in other words pursuing righteousness, he is carrying out the will and intention of that Divine Being whom we here call Nature but whom we might also call God.

This, or something like it, is the ideal of a man which most of us would form under the impress and impetus of the indwelling genius of Nature. But this ideal can only be reached by an individual when his country also has reached it. He will be driven, therefore, to make his country behave and act up to this ideal. And his country cannot so act till the general society of nations conducts itself on the same general lines. His country, therefore, will be driven to make the general society of nations behave in accordance with the principles of high fellowship.

* * *

We have made for ourselves the ideal of a man. It remains to show that the finest pitch of all is only reached in the union of man and woman. The man is not complete without the woman, nor the woman without the man. It is in their union, therefore, that the ideal in its greatest perfection will be seen. The flower which results from the working of the ideal in the Heart of Nature, as the flower of the rose results from the working of the rose-ideal in the heart of the rose-seed, we see in the love of man and woman at the supreme moment of their union. This is the very holiest thing in Nature. It is then that both the man and the woman are to the fullest extent themselves, both to be and to express all that is in them to be. They love then to their extreme capacity to love. They are gentle then to the utmost limit of tenderness. And they are strong then to the farthest stretch of their strength.

And while they thus reach the very acme of Nature's ideal so far as we men can discern it, they, at the same time and in so doing, touch the very foundations of Nature as well. Mathematicians have discovered that there is no such thing as a perfectly straight line, and that curvature is a fundamental property of the physical world. So also is it in the spiritual world. As we reach the topmost height of the ideal we find that it has curved round, and that we are at that moment at the very base and foundation. What is attracting us forward in the farthest distance in front is the very thing that is urging us forward from behind. Pinnacle and foundation, source and end, meet.

The love which attracted the man and woman together and which they keep striving to attain in higher and higher degree, is the same as the creative impulse which comes surging up from the very Heart of Nature. Direct and without ever a break it has come out of the remotest past and deepest deeps. Few seem aware of this, and yet it is an obvious fact—and a fact which vastly increases our sense of intimacy with Nature. It was due to the same impulse which has brought the man and woman together that they themselves were brought into being. Their parents had been attracted by the same vision of love and impelled by the same impulse. Their parents' parents had been similarly attracted and impelled, and so on back and back through the whole long line of ancestry, through half a million years to primitive men, back beyond them again through the long animal ancestry for scores of millions of years to the beginning of life. Even then there is no break. Direct from the very Fountain Source of Things this creative impulse has come bursting up into their hearts. At the moment of union they are straight along the direct line of the whole world-development, so far as this planet is concerned. The elemental in the natural impulse is the most ultimately elemental, for it derives itself straight from the pure Origin of Things. As they reach after the most Divine they are impelled by the most elemental. What, in fact, happens is that the elemental is inspired through and through with the Divine.

The union of man and woman is the flower of Nature. But, like the rose, it bears within it the seed from which some still more beautiful flower may result. No pair, however sublime their union, suppose that it is the best that could by any possibility at any time exist. An absolutely perfect union depends upon an absolutely perfect pair in absolutely perfect surroundings. And no one supposes that he himself is perfect or that the world around him is perfect. So there is in the pair a consciousness of imperfection, a vision of perfection, and a desperate yearning to be more perfect and to make the world more perfect. Deep and strong as the creative impulse itself is the impulse to improvement. It is due to this impulse that the mother reaches over her child with such loving care, strives to shield it from all harm, social as well as physical, and to give it a better chance than she herself enjoyed. It is due to this same impulse that the man works to leave his profession, his business, his science, his art, his country, better than he found it. It is due to this impulse also that men as a whole are driven to improve the whole Earth, to improve plants, flowers, trees, animals, men, and make the world a better place for their successors than it has ever been for them.

The pair—even the most splendid pair that has ever wedded—have deep within them this perhaps unrecognised impulse to improvement. They know that the rose can only bring forth roses, and that they can only bring forth men: they know that they cannot bring forth angels. But they know also that the rose, when wisely mated and its offspring provided with favourable surroundings of soil and air and sunshine, can give rise to blooms incomparably more perfect than itself. And they know that they themselves, if they have wisely mated, if they carefully tend their offspring and provide them with healthy, sunny, physical and social surroundings, can give rise, in generations to come, to unions of men and women incomparably more perfect than their own—as much more perfect as their union is than the unions of primitive men—richer in colour, more graceful in form, sweeter in fragrance, and of an altogether finer texture.

* * *

This, then, is the ideal in its completeness which we set up before us. But we have no sooner set it up than we find that the presence of this ideal within us makes us restless, unsatisfied, discontented, till we have set to work to bring things up to it; and that when we do start improving them we are forthwith involved in endless strife. Improvement means effort. It does not come by itself. It is only effected by strong, persistent, determined effort. It was no easy matter for the particles in the rose-seed to battle their way through the hard seed-case, strike down into the soil, send up shoots into the air, stand steadfastly to their ideal of the rose, and produce a seed capable of bringing forth a still more perfect flower. And it is no easy matter for us to burst through our own shells, strike our roots far down into the soil of common humanity and common animality, and there firmly rooted strike up skyward, stand faithfully to our ideal, and produce something which will have capacity for still further improvement. Immense and sustained effort is required of us for this to be accomplished.

Each man finds he has to battle with himself to make way for all the best in himself to come to the front. Each has to battle with the circumstances in which he is placed in order to find scope for the exercise of the best in himself. Each has to break his way through, as that wonder of Nature, poor primitive man, had to battle his way through the impediments of the tropical forests and the brute beasts by which he was surrounded. And just as primitive man was not the animal provided with the thickest hide like the rhinoceros, nor with sharpest claws like the lion, nor with the fiercest temper like the tiger, but was of all his fellows the one with the most sensitive nature, so are those nearest the ideal the most delicately sensitive of mankind.

The ideal is never approached, much less attained, except by men and women of the most highly-strung natures—natures peculiarly susceptible to pain. And with this extra susceptibility to pain they have to expose to the risk of wounds and bruises the most sensitive parts of their natures. Suffering is therefore inevitably their lot. It is the invariable attendant of progress however beneficent. Excruciating pain each expects to have to endure—as every expectant mother and every soldier anticipates on the physical plane.

We find, too, that in working out our ideal we are not only required to endure pain, but to submit to the sternest discipline. First, we need self-discipline. Each individual finds that he is required to exercise his faculties to the full, make the utmost of himself, attain to the highest of which he is capable, and be ready for any sacrifice. So he must train his faculties to the highest. He is required also to work in concert with his fellows. The stern obligation is therefore upon him to forgo his own private advantage in order that the common end may be achieved. This obligation he has readily to acknowledge and submit to. He has also to acknowledge what he owes to Nature, what is his *duty* to Nature. And that duty he has to perform and her authority he has to admit. He can retain his freedom and initiative and enterprise. But he has to obey the laws of Nature, acknowledge her authority, submit to her discipline. No soldiers were more full of independence and initiative than the Australians, but no troops at the end of the War realised better than they did that success can only be achieved through strictest discipline as well as freedom and initiative. The lover also knows that only through the sternest discipline and constraint upon himself is his object attained. Thus there is an imperative necessity upon a man to be orderly in his behaviour, loyal, faithful, dutiful, and obedient to the ideal within him. Any failure in loyalty and obedience is a sin against Nature and a sin against himself. The call of honour and of humanity is upon him, and that call he has to obey without hesitation.

Equally are men expected to be ready to *exercise* authority, to maintain discipline and preserve order. The exercise of authority is no less an obligation and duty upon men than obedience to it. And the one has to be practised just as much as the other. Or, rather, the exercise of authority has to be practised more, for it is more difficult and more valuable. And the proper exercise of authority, maintenance of discipline, and preservation of order, is a duty men owe ultimately to Nature herself. For it is from Nature that they finally derive their authority and to Nature that they are ultimately responsible.

Whether as captain of the eleven or as head of the house at school, as manager of an office or a business, as policeman or foreman, as corporal or Commander-in-Chief, as administrator or Prime Minister, whether as nurse, parent, or schoolmistress, a man or woman is in his position of authority directly or indirectly on the appointment or choice of those over whom he has to exercise authority. He is there to exercise authority for their benefit. They have placed him—as the public place the policeman—in authority for that purpose. And they have a right to expect that he will exercise his authority with decision, maintain discipline with firmness, and preserve order with even-handed justice. For only then can they themselves know where they are, get on with their own duties and affairs, and fulfil the law of their being. Ultimately those in authority are chosen by, and are responsible to, those over whom they exercise authority. And those who choose them expect and require them to exercise authority authoritatively.

Each in his own particular sphere, in that particular place and for the time being, has to exercise his authority with strictness. Otherwise the rest cannot fulfil their own duties. The policeman has to exercise his authority even over a Prince, as otherwise there might be chaos in the streets and no one would be able to get about his business with surety. The whole people have chosen each for his particular position of authority, and for their benefit expect him to exercise it strictly.

The people, again, spring from Nature as a whole. They are the representatives of Nature. Those in authority are therefore, in their particular province, for that particular purpose, and for the time being the representatives of Nature. They are accountable to Nature, and Nature expects them as her representatives to exercise authority with wisdom and discretion, but on the same basic principles of absolute fairness and perfect orderliness that she herself in her elemental aspects exercises her authority.

Besides obeying authority and exercising authority, men have also to practise *leadership*. Merely to give and obey orders is nothing like sufficient. In most things a man follows some leader, but in each man there is one thing—his own particular line—in which he can *lead*. In that line he is expected to qualify himself for leadership, and be prepared to take the risks of high adventure. For it is only through leadership, through someone venturing out beyond the ruck and getting his fellows to follow him, that any progress is made. Mere obedience to authority and exercise of authority never initiate any new departure. These only provide the conditions for progress. In addition to these the divine gift of leadership is required. Leadership is therefore the supremely important quality which men require.

But men cannot intelligently act in concert and alertly; cannot willingly submit themselves to a rigid discipline; cannot exercise authority with confidence and weight; and cannot lead so that others may follow, unless all are animated by the same idea. And they are not likely to sacrifice their lives for that idea unless they are convinced of its value. Only for the most precious things in life do men willingly give up their lives. And before they submit to unquestioning discipline and sacrifice themselves for an ideal they need a clear understanding of that ideal and a just appreciation of its value. So they think out the ideal with greater precision and make sure that what they are aiming at is nothing short of the highest. Now the ideal of fellowship enriched with beauty and elevated to the Divine is one which all can understand and of which all can see the value. Because it is the highest it is satisfying to the deepest needs and cravings of their nature, and is therefore of a value beyond all reckoning. Assured of that, they summon up all the courage and fortitude that is theirs, all their spirit and mettle, to endure unflinchingly the pain that must be theirs. And in spite of the effort, the long, strict training, the rigid discipline, the hardship and suffering they have to undergo, they joyfully play their part because they are assured in their hearts that what they are living for and would readily die for is supremely worth while. Deep in their hearts is that divine joy of battle that fighters for the highest always feel. And they fight with power and conviction because they know that their ideal has come into their hearts straight from Nature herself, and experience has shown that what Nature has in mind she does in the end achieve: she not only has the will and intention but the *power* to carry into effect what she determines.

* * *

This is how we formulate the ideal to ourselves in ever-developing completeness; and this is how with pain and effort but with over-compensating joy we carry it into effect. And these experiences of ours in the formulation and working out of our ideal give us the clue to the manner in which Nature on her part works out *her* ideal. We are the representations and representatives of the whole, and we may assume that the whole works in much the same way as we ourselves work. If this be so we may expect to find that Nature will work as an *artist* works, that is, out of his own inner consciousness, spontaneously generating and continually creating new and original forms approaching (through a process of trial and error experimentation) more and more closely to that ideal of perfection which he has always, though often unconsciously, before him. And this is how we actually do find Nature working. We find her reaching after perfection of form, now in one direction, now in another; first in plants, next in animals, then in insects, then in birds, then in apes, then in men, here in one type and there in another, never reaching complete perfection anywhere, any more than the greatest artist ever does in any particular, but still reaching perfection in a higher and higher degree, and making the state of the whole of a richer and intenser perfection.

We have, therefore, ample evidence that Nature is actuated by an intention to enrich perfection and is continually working towards it. So we have confidence that Nature, hard and exacting though she be, is *only* exacting in order that the Highest may be attained. We know that Nature is aiming at the Highest and nothing short of the Highest. And all the spirit of daring and adventure in us leaps to the call she makes.

And we respond to the call with all the greater alacrity because we feel that the attainment of that Highest is dependent to a large degree upon ourselves. We have a sense of real responsibility in the matter. And for this reason—that though Nature lays down the great constitutional laws within which man, her completest representative, must work; and though Nature as a whole formulates the main outlines of her ideal; yet man *within that constitution* can make his own laws, and within its main outlines may refine and perfect the ideal.

Nature may be working out her ideal on other stars through the agency of other kinds of beings more perfect than ourselves; and while the ideal in its main outlines may be the same there as the ideal which is working itself out on this planet, it may there have assumed a higher form and be more nearly attained. But on this planet the more definite formulation of the ideal and the measures for its attainment are in the hands of men. We can perfect the ideal for ourselves, and make laws and establish customs to ensure its attainment. We are not the slaves of a despotic ruler, or pawns in the hand of an external player. Within the limits of Nature's constitution, the laws we obey are laws of our own making; the authority we obey is the authority which we ourselves have set up; and both authority and laws we can change in accordance with the growing requirements of the ideal which we ourselves are perfecting.

We go forward, therefore, with inextinguishable faith in the value of what we are battling for, and in the worthwhileness of all our efforts and endurances. And though the ideal, with which Nature has inspired us makes us restless and discontented, provokes us to increasing effort, causes us endless pain and suffering, and exacts from us the sacrifice even of our lives, we nevertheless love to have the ideal, and love Nature for implanting it in us.

* * *

And now that we have seen what is the nature of Nature, what is the end she has before her, and how she works to accomplish her end, we feel that we have gone a long way towards knowing and understanding her. We have had a vision of the hidden Divinity by which she is inspired. And this mysterious Power we have not found reigning remote in the empty spaces of the heavens. We have found it dwelling in every minutest particle of which this Earth and all the world is built, and of which we ourselves also are made—dwelling in the earth, and in the air, and in the stars; and in every living thing, in beast and bird and insect, in flower, plant, and man—and dwelling in them all in their togetherness. We have found it to be both immanent and transcendent. It only exists—and can only exist—in these its single self-active representations. But in relation to each of them it is transcendent. Each star and flower, each beast and man, is its partial representation. But the whole together is that Power which while it transcends is yet resident in, and inspires, each single part which goes to its making. In the inmost heart of Nature, as the ground and source of Nature, yet permeating Nature to the uttermost confines, and reigning supreme over the whole, we find God; actuating the heart of God we find an ideal; and actuating the heart of the ideal we find an imperative urge towards perfection, an inborn necessity to perfect itself for ever—just as inside the rough exterior of Abraham Lincoln was the real Abraham Lincoln, at his heart was an ideal, and at the heart of the ideal an inner impulse towards perfection; or as within the exterior France is the real France, in the heart of France an ideal, and in the heart of the ideal the determination to perfect itself.

This view of Nature is very different from that view of her which would regard the world as having been originally created by, and now being governed by, an always and already perfect Being, living as apart from it as the Sun is from the Earth, and being as distinct and separate from it as a father is from his son. And the difference in view must make a profound difference in our attitude to Nature, and therefore in our capacity for seeing and enjoying Natural Beauty. We may admire and worship but we can scarcely love, in any true sense of the word, a Being dwelling distant and aloof from us, and with whom, from the mere fact of his being perfect, it is most difficult for us to be on terms of homely intimacy and affection. But for a Being who, like our country, is one of whom we ourselves form part, we can have not only admiration and reverence but deep affection. We can and do love our country, for we form part of her, and have a voice and share in making and shaping her. We know that she cares for us, will look after us in misfortune, and will honour and love us if we serve her well and show her loyalty and devotion. And we can and do love Nature for precisely the same reasons. We feel ourselves part of her, and in intimate touch with her all round and always. And we have that which is so satisfying to us—the feeling that there is *reciprocity* of love between us and her. So our love is active, and it vehemently impels us to get to know her better and better, to get ourselves in ever closer touch with her, to discover the utmost fulness of her Beauty, and to communicate to others all that we have come to know and all the Beauty we have seen, so that others may share in our enjoyment and come to love Nature more even than we love her ourselves—love Nature in all her aspects, love physical Nature in the mountains, seas and deserts, the clouds, sunsets and stars, love plant Nature and animal Nature and human Nature; and, above all, love Divine Nature as best revealed in supreme men in their supreme moments.

In some of her aspects Nature may be stern and exacting. But she is never sheerly hard. She is compounded of mercy and compassion as well as of rigid orderliness. And her essential character is Love—and Love of no impassive and insipid kind, but of a power and activity beyond all human conception.

The importance and significance of this conclusion, if we accept it, is that we definitely abandon the repellent conception of Nature as governed by chance, or as cold and mechanical, or as guided solely by the principle of the survival of the fittest, and we accept instead the humaner and diviner view that Nature is actuated by Love; and, accepting that more winning conception, we can enter unreservedly into the Spirit of Nature and see her Beauty. Unless we had been assured in our minds, without any possibility of doubt whatever, that we could *love* Nature, we could never really have enjoyed her *Beauty*.

* * *

So Nature is not something static, fixed, and immovable, determined once and for all like a rock is, at least to outward appearance. Nature is a Person, and a Person is a process. Nature flows. Nature is always moving on. As our thoughts are all connected with one another and passing into one another; as all events are connected with one another and are continually passing from one into another, and form one great all-inclusive event which is in continual process of happening; so is Nature always in process of passing from one state into another state, while the whole forms one great event for ever happening. And actuating the whole process, determining the whole great event, is an inner core of Activity which endures through all the changes. It is the "I" of Nature, which informs, directs, controls the whole from centre to utmost extremity through all space and all time. It is the Soul and Spirit, the Genius of Nature. It is what we should mean when we speak of God.

Actuated by this spirit, whose essential character is Love, the process glides smoothly, unbrokenly, and wellnigh imperceptibly forward. As we lift our eyes and look out upon Nature in its present actually existing state, what we see in that instant is the whole achievement of the past, and it contains within it here and now the promise of all the future. All the past is in the present, and in it also is the potency of the future. The achievement fills us with admiration. The promise thrills us with hope. To that Spirit which has achieved this result, which actuates the process and ourselves with it, which determines the great event, which ensures the uniformity and law and order which are the foundations of our freedom, and the essential condition of all progress, our hearts are drawn out and yearningly stretch themselves out in a love boundless as the process itself.

The more we find ourselves drawn to Nature and in harmony and love with her, the more Beauty do we see. In closest reciprocity Love of Nature inspires Natural Beauty and Natural Beauty promotes Love of Nature. And it is from the Heart of Nature that both Love and Beauty spring. Both also remain permanent and everlasting through all the changing processes of Nature—permanent but ever increasing in depth and height and volume. The promise of all the Love and Beauty of to-day was hidden in the womb of the past. In the womb of to-day is contained the promise of a Love and Beauty still more glorious. And ours it is to bring them into being.

PART II.
NATURAL BEAUTY AND GEOGRAPHY

PRESIDENTIAL ADDRESS TO THE ROYAL GEOGRAPHICAL SOCIETY, DELIVERED AT THE ANNIVERSARY MEETING, MAY 31, 1920

NATURAL BEAUTY AND GEOGRAPHICAL SCIENCE

I have something to say which to old-fashioned geographers may appear very revolutionary, and which you may hesitate to accept straight away. But it has come to me as the result of much and varied geographical work in the field; of listening to many lectures before this Society; and of composing this Address and five lectures for you, firstly, as far back as 1888, on my journey across Central Asia from Peking to India; secondly, on my journey to Hunza and the Pamirs; thirdly, on Chitral; fourthly, on my mission to Tibet; and fifthly, on the Himalaya. And I expect when you come to think over what I have now to say you will find that, after all, my conclusions are not anything desperately revolutionary but something quite obvious and natural.

What I want to lay before you for your very earnest consideration is this—that we should take a profounder and broader view of Geography, of its fundamental conception, and of its scope and aim, than we have hitherto taken; and should regard the Earth as *Mother*-Earth, and the *Beauty* of her features as within the purview of Geography.

I will state my case as clearly and briefly as I can. Geography is a science. Science is learning, knowing, understanding. The object of geographical learning, knowing, understanding is the Earth. We must first, then, have a true conception of what the Earth really is. And next we must be certain in our minds as to what is most worth knowing about it.

To begin with our conception of the Earth. At the dawn of Geography it was believed to be a flat disc. Later it was discovered to be a sphere. Then it was found to be not a hard solid sphere like a billiard-ball, but to be hard only on the surface, and within to be quick with fervent heat. Now it is coming to be regarded as spirit as well as body—as in its essential nature spiritual rather than material.

When we get as far back as science is able to take us we find that the ultimate particles of which the Earth is made up are not minute specks of some substance or material, but are simply centres of radiant energy. Even with a microscope of infinite power we should never be able to see one, like we see a grain of pollen or a grain of sand. And if we had fingers of infinite delicacy, we should never be able to take one up between the forefinger and thumb and feel it. These ultimate particles are invisible and intangible. Nothing could be less substantial. And we find further that, inconceivably minute as they are, they *act of themselves* under the mutual influence of one another. The electrons are not like shot which have been heaped together by some outside agency, and which roll about the floor if someone outside gives them a push, but which will otherwise remain immobile. They congregate together of their own inner prompting. They are like a swarm of midges or bees in which each individual acts on its own impulsion, and, in the case of bees, all together form themselves into a definite organisation with a collective spirit of its own. The Earth is indeed influenced by its parent the Sun, and acts in accordance with the same laws and is swayed by the same impulses as govern the whole Universe, of which it is a minute though highly important mite. But the point is that the Earth is not something like a lump of clay which a potter takes in his hands and moulds into a ball. The Earth moulds itself from activities that it contains within itself.

Running through the whole mighty swarm of electrons we call the Earth is a tendency to order, organisation, and system. The myriad millions of ultimate particles in their all-togetherness and from their interaction upon one another become possessed of an imperative urge towards excellence. The electrons group themselves into atoms; the atoms clump themselves together into molecules; the molecules combine into chemical compounds, and these into organisms of ever-increasing size and complexity. So in the process of the ages there came into being, from out of the very Earth itself, first, lowly forms of plants and animals, then higher and higher forms exhibiting higher and higher qualities, till the flowers of the field, the animals, and man himself came into existence.

And now we reach the point I wish to make. If this account of the Earth which physicists and biologists give us be true, then we geographers should take a less material and a more spiritual view of the Earth than we have done, and should, like primitive people all the world over, regard her as Mother-

Earth, and recognise our intimate connection with her. Primitive peoples everywhere regard the Earth as alive and as their Mother. And so intensely do they feel this liveness that many will not run the plough through the soil from dislike of lacerating the bosom of Mother-Earth. They see plants and trees spring up out of her, and these plants and trees providing them with fruits and seeds, leaves and roots, upon which to live. And they quite naturally look upon her as their Mother. And we men of the more advanced races have still more cause to consider her as our Mother, for we now know that not only the plants and trees but we ourselves sprang from her—as indeed we are nourished by her daily, eating her plants or the animals which feed on her plants. And as we judge of a lily, not by its origin, the ugly bulb, but by the climax, the exquisite flower; so we should not judge of the Earth by its origin, the fiery mist, but by its issue—ardent human fellowship. And if we thus judge her we shall find her a mother worthy of our affection.

So the first point I have to put before you is that we geographers should regard the object of our science not as a magnified billiard-ball, but as a living being—as Mother-Earth. Not as hard, unimpressionable, dull, and inert, but as live, supple, sensitive, and active—active with an intensity of activity past all conceivability. Yet with no chaotic activity, but with activity having coherence and direction, and that direction towards excellence.

* * *

Now as to what we ought to know about the Earth. While Geology concerns itself with its anatomy, Geography, by long convention, restricts its concern to the Earth's outward aspect. Accordingly, it is in the face and features of Mother-Earth that we geographers are mainly interested. We must know something of the general principles of geology, as painters have to know something of the anatomy of the human or animal body. But our special business as geographers is with the outward expression. And my second point is that the characteristic of the face and features of the Earth most worth learning about, knowing, and understanding is their Beauty; and that knowledge of their Beauty may be legitimately included within the scope of geographical science.

It may be argued, indeed, that science is concerned with quantity—with what can be measured—and that Natural Beauty is quality which is something that eludes measurement. But geographical science, at least, should refuse to be confined within any such arbitrary limits and should take cognisance of quality as well as quantity. This is my contention. I am not maintaining that the actual enjoyment of the Natural Beauty of the Earth should be regarded as within the scope of geographical science, though this Society as a social body might well participate in such enjoyment. Enjoyment is feeling, whereas science is knowing; and feeling and knowing are distinct faculties. We can easily see the distinction. We may be travelling to Plymouth to embark for South Africa on some absorbing enterprise, and be so engrossed with thoughts of the adventure before us as to be unable to enjoy the famed West Country through which the train is passing, though all the time we were quite aware in our minds of its beauty. We are not actually enjoying the beauty, though we know quite well that it is there. On another occasion we may be returning after long absence in countries of far different character; our minds may be free from any disturbing thoughts; and we may be in a mood to enjoy to the full every beauty we see. England will then seem to us a veritable garden, the greenness of everything, the trimness of the hedges, the sheets of purple hyacinths, and some still remaining primroses, will startle us with joy, though we have long been aware of their beauty. This time we both know and enjoy the Natural Beauty. We see from this instance the distinction between knowing Natural Beauty and enjoying it. I am not claiming more than that *knowing* Natural Beauty—being aware of it—is part of Geography. But I *am* claiming liberty to extend our knowing up to the extreme limit when it merges into feeling.

What we have now to consider is the value of this Natural Beauty. A region may be flat or mountainous, dry or wet, barren or fertile, useful or useless for either political or commercial purposes. But it is not its flatness or ruggedness, or its utility or inutility for political or commercial purposes, that we may find in the end is the most noteworthy characteristic, but its beauty— its own particular beauty. The conventional gold or oil prospector, or railway engineer, or seeker for sites for rubber or coffee plantation, or pasture-lands for sheep and cattle, may not bother his head about the beauty of the forests, the rivers, the prairies, and the mountains he is exploring. He is much too absorbed in the practical business of life to be distracted by anything so fanciful—as he thinks. Yet even he does see the beauty, and long afterwards he finds it is that which has stuck most firmly in his mind. And when he has unthinkingly destroyed it, future generations lament his action and take measures to preserve what remains. Advertisements, also, show us daily that nearly all countries—and it seems more especially new countries like Canada and New Zealand—regard Natural Beauty as one of their most valuable assets. And the reason why the Natural Beauty of the Earth is deemed so valuable a characteristic of its features is not hard to understand when we come to reflect. It is because Beauty is a quality which appeals to the universal in man—appeals to all men for all time, and appeals to them in an increasing degree. It is something which all men can admire and enjoy. And the more they enjoy it the more they want to get others to share in their enjoyment. Also the more Natural Beauty they see, the more, apparently, there is to see.

Poets in their poems, and painters in their pictures, are continually pointing out to us less keen-sighted individuals new beauties in the features of the Earth. The mineral wealth of the Earth has its limits; even the productivity, though perennially renewed, is not unbounded. But the Natural Beauty is inexhaustible. And it is not only inexhaustible: it positively increases and multiplies the more we see of it and the more of us see it. So it has good claim to be considered the most valuable characteristic of the Earth.

And if Beauty should prove to be its most valuable characteristic, it follows that knowledge of it is the knowledge about the Earth which is most worth having. It will certainly be the case that knowledge of other characteristics may be of more value to particular men for a special purpose for the time being. If an engineer has to build a railway, knowledge of the exact height above sea-level of various points and of the general configuration of the ground is of more value than knowledge of its beauty. But for the engineer himself, when he is not thinking of his railway, and for mankind in general, knowledge of the beauty may be the more valuable kind of knowledge.

For years I was employed in exploring the region where three Empires meet, where the Himalaya, the Hindu Kush, and mountains which form the Roof of the World converge. I had to report on the extent to which it afforded a barrier against the advance of Russia towards India, and wherein it would lie the most appropriate boundary between India and Russia, between India and China, and between Russia and China. What I learned of that region as a barrier against invasion was of more value to the Viceroy and Commander-in-Chief in India and the political and military authorities in England in the discharge of their official duties than what I learned of its beauties. But this utility of the region as a military barrier is not the characteristic which has most value to men in general. What to them has most value is its beauty—the awful beauty of its terrific gorges and stupendous heights. And it is knowledge of this beauty which is most worth having, and which has most geographical value.

Besides exploring the far region beyond Kashmir I was also employed for years in exercising a general supervision over the entire administration of Kashmir itself. Reports from experts used to come to me containing every description of geographical knowledge. Surveyors would send in maps for general purposes, for the construction of roads and railways, for the delimitation of village boundaries, and for registering the ownership of individual fields. Geologists would report on the crustal relief (as the features of Mother-Earth are inelegantly termed). Forestry, agricultural, and botanical experts would report on the productivity of the soil, on the plants and trees which are or might be grown, and on their present and possible distribution.

Mineralogists would report on the minerals, their distribution and the possibility of commercially exploiting them. Every aspect of geographical science was presented to me. And each particular kind of knowledge for its own particular purpose was highly valuable. But the point I would wish to make is that my geographical knowledge of Kashmir would have been incomplete—and I would have been wanting in knowledge of its most valuable characteristic—if I had had no knowledge of its beauty. I might have had the most precise knowledge about the form and structure of the crustal relief of this portion of the Earth, of the productivity of the soil, of the distribution of its population, and of animals and plants, and about the effect of the crustal forms on the animals and plants, and of the animals and plants upon the crustal forms and of all upon man, and of man upon them all; but if I had had no knowledge of the beauty of these crustal forms and of the influence which their beauty has upon man, I should not have known what was most worth knowing about Kashmir. My geographical knowledge of that country would have been wanting in its most important particular.

These illustrations will, I hope, make clear what I mean when I urge that Beauty may be the most valuable characteristic of the Earth's features, and that the scope of Geography should certainly be extended to include a knowledge of it.

And there should be less hesitation in accepting the latter half of this conclusion when we note that Natural Beauty affects the movements of man, and that man is having an increasing effect upon Natural Beauty—spoiling it in too many cases, improving it in many others, but certainly having an effect upon it. There is thus a quite definite relation between man and Natural Beauty, and it should therefore be within the scope of Geography to take note of this relationship. To an increasing degree man now moves about in search of new Natural Beauty or to enjoy it where it has been already found. From all over the world men flock to Switzerland, drawn there by its beauty. Here at home they go to the Thames Valley, or Dartmoor, or the coast of Cornwall, or North Wales, or the Highlands, simply to enjoy the Natural Beauty. And railway companies and the Governments of Canada, Australia, and New Zealand think it worth while to spend large sums of money in publishing pictures of the beauty of the countries in which they are interested in order to attract holiday-makers or home-seekers to them.

And here, as in other cases, man now is not content to be an impassive spectator and to be entirely controlled by his surroundings. He does not allow the "crustal relief" to have the upper hand in the matter. He will not admit that all he has to do is to adapt himself to his surroundings. That servile view of our position in the Universe is fast departing. We are determined to have the ascendancy. And much as we admire the Beauty of the Earth we set about improving it. We fail disastrously at times, I allow. But sometimes unconsciously, and sometimes deliberately, we succeed. We have in places made the Earth more beautiful than it was before we came, and we have certainly shown the possibility of this being done. From what I have seen in uninhabited countries I can realise what the river-valleys of England must have been like before the arrival of man—beautiful, certainly; but not *so* beautiful as now. They must have been an unrelieved mass of forest and marsh. Now the marshes are drained and turned into golden meadows. The woods are cleared in part and well-kept parks take their place, with trees specially selected, pruned, and trim, and made to stand out well by themselves so that their umbrageous forms may be properly seen. Gardens are laid out, the famous lawns of England are created, and flowering and variegated shrubs from many lands are planted round them. And homes are built—the simple homes of the poor and the stately homes of the rich—which in the setting of trees and lawns and gardens add unquestionably to the natural beauty of the land. St. James's Park, with its lake, its well-tended trees, its daisy-covered lawns, its flowerbeds, its may and lilac, laburnum and horse-chestnut, and with the towers of Westminster Abbey and the Houses of Parliament rising behind it, is certainly more beautiful than the same piece of land was two thousand years ago in its natural condition.

What has been done in this respect in England is only typical of what is done in every country and of what has been done for ages past. The Moghul emperors, by the planting of gardens on the borders of the Dal Lake in Kashmir, added greatly to its beauty. And the Japanese are famous for the choice of beautiful surroundings for their temples and for the addition which they themselves, by the erection of graceful temples and by properly cared-for trees and gardens, make to the natural beauty of the place.

So man is both affected by the Beauty of the Earth's features and himself affects that Beauty. And this relationship between man and the Natural Beauty of the Earth is one of which Geography should take as much cognisance as it does of the relationship between man and the productivity of the Earth.

But Natural Beauty is manifested in an innumerable variety of forms. The whole Beauty is never manifested in any one particular feature or region, but each has its unique aspect. Each feature has its own peculiar beauty different from the beauty of any other feature. And what men naturally do, and what I would suggest geographers should deliberately do, is to compare the beauty of one region with the beauty of another, so that we may realise the beauty of each with a greater intensity and clearness. We can compare the beauty of Kashmir with the beauty of Switzerland and California. And the comparison will enable us to see more clearly and to appreciate the distinctive elements which make up the peculiar beauty of each of those countries. It has been frequently noticed that people who have always lived in the same place are unable to see its full beauty. The inhabitants of the Gilgit frontier, when I first went among them, had never left their mountains, and were altogether ignorant of the special grandeur of their beauty. They thought all the world was just the same. But men who have seen many varieties of Natural Beauty and have taken pains to compare the varieties with one another become trained to see more Beauty in each feature. Fresh discoveries of Beauty are thus made, and our knowledge of the Beauty of the Earth is thereby increased.

* * *

What I hope, then, is that this Society should definitely recognise that learning to see the Beauty in natural features and comparing the peculiar beauties of the different features with one another is within the scope of Geography, and will indeed become its chief function. I should like to see the tradition established and well known and recognised that we encourage the search for Natural Beauty, and look upon the discovery of a new region which possesses special beauty, and the discovery of a new beauty in a region already well known, as among the most important geographical discoveries to be made. In this matter I trust our Society will take the lead. Englishmen are born lovers of Natural Beauty and born travellers. The search for Natural Beauty ought, therefore, to be a congenial task for this Society. As I have tried to make clear, we cannot really know and understand the Earth—which is the aim of Geography—until we have seen its beauties and compared the varying beauties of the different features with one another and seen how they affect man and man affects them. We are constituted as a Society for the purpose of diffusing geographical knowledge, and I trust that in future we shall regard knowledge of the Beauty of the Earth as the most important form of geographical knowledge that we can diffuse.

When I was Writing out the lecture which I was invited to give before the Society on "The Geographical Results of the Tibet Mission" I could not resist devoting special attention to the natural beauty of Tibet. But as I read the manuscript through I feared that this attention to Beauty would be regarded by our Society as a lapse from the narrow path of pure Geography, and that I should be frowned upon in consequence and not regarded as a serious geographer. I ought, I feared, to have devoted more attention to survey matters, to the exact trend of the mountains, and the source and course of the rivers. But looking back now I see that my natural instinct was a right one—that a knowledge of the beauties of Tibet was not only one geographical result of the Mission, but the chief geographical result; and that, in fact, I ought to have paid not less but more attention, both in Tibet to noting its beauties in all their multitudinous variety, and in writing my lecture to expressing with point and precision what I had seen, so that you might share it with me, and learn what is the most valuable characteristic of Tibet.

When the new tradition is established, and travellers become aware that we regard knowledge of Natural Beauty as within the scope of our activities, the error into which I fell will be avoided. We shall think travellers barbaric if they continue to concern themselves with all else about the face of the Earth except its Beauty. We shall no longer tolerate a geographer who will learn everything about the utility of a region for military, political, and commercial purposes, but who will take no trouble to see the beauty it contains. We shall expect a much higher standard of him. We shall expect him to cultivate the power of the eye till he has a true eye for country—a seeing eye; an eye that can see into the very heart and, through all the thronging details, single out the one essential quality; an eye which can not only observe but can make discoveries. We shall require him to have the capacity for discriminating the essential from the unessential, for bringing that essential into proper relief and placing upon it the due emphasis. When he thus has true vision and can really see a country, and when he has acquired the capacity for expressing either in words or in painting what lie has seen, so that he can communicate it to us, then he will have reached the standard which this Society should demand. And this is nothing less than saying that we expect of him that he should have in him something of the poet and the painter.

Careless snap-shotting in the field and idle turning on of lantern slides at our meetings will no longer satisfy us. A traveller if he is going to photograph must spend the hours which a real artist would devote to discovering the essential beauty of a scene, and to composing his picture before he dreams of exposing his plate. But we want more than photographs: we want pictures to give that important element in Natural Beauty—the colour. And we want pictures painted in words as well as on canvas. Not shallow rhapsodising of the journalese and guide-book type, but true expression in which each noun exactly fits the object, each epithet is truly applicable, and each phrase is rightly turned, and in which the emphasis is placed on the precisely right point, and the whole composed so as distinctly to bring out that point.

Then in time we shall gather together the most valuable knowledge about the Earth. And when a stranger from a far land comes to us to know about any particular country, we shall be able to provide him with something worth having. When an Australian comes to England and wishes to know its essential characteristics, we shall do something more than hand him over maps and treatises on the orography and hydrography, the distribution of rainfall, of plants and animals, and the population. We shall regard ourselves as having omitted to point out to him the essential characteristic of the land from which Englishmen have sprung and in which they dwell if we have not shown him the beauty of its natural features. We shall give him the maps as aids to finding his way about, and we shall give him the treatises. But we shall tell him that these are only aids for special purposes, and that if he is really to understand England he must know its beauty in its many aspects. He will then have the geographical knowledge of chief value about England.

* * *

A project in which the Society is now interested affords an excellent opportunity of applying the principles I have been trying to persuade you to adopt. The most prominent feature of this Earth, and the feature of most geographical interest, is the great range of the Himalaya Mountains. In this range the supreme summit is Mount Everest, the highest point on the Earth, 29,002 feet above sea-level. Attempts have been made to ascend the second highest mountain, K2, 28,278 feet, notably by the Duke of the Abruzzi. Colonel Hon. Charles Bruce, Major Rawling, and others have had in mind the idea of ascending Mount Everest itself. And for more than a year past both the Alpine Club and this Society have been definitely entertaining the idea of helping forward the achievement of this object. We hope within the next few years to hear of a human being standing on the pinnacle of the Earth.

If I am asked, What is the use of climbing this highest mountain? I reply, No use at all: no more use than kicking a football about, or dancing, or playing on the piano, or writing a poem, or painting a picture. The geologist predicts to a certainty that no gold will be found on the summit, and if gold did exist there no one would be able to work it. Climbing Mount Everest will not put a pound into anyone's pocket. It will take a good many pounds out of people's pockets. It will also entail the expenditure of much time and necessitate the most careful forethought and planning on the part of those who are organising the expedition. And it will mean that those who carry it out will have to keep themselves at the very highest pitch of physical fitness, mental alertness, and moral courage and endurance. They will have to be prepared to undergo the severest hardships and run considerable risks. And all this, I say, without the prospect of making a single penny. So there will be no *use* in climbing Mount Everest. If the ascent is made at all it will be made for the sheer love of the thing, from pure enjoyment—the enjoyment a man gets from pitting himself against a big obstacle.

But if there is no *use,* there is unquestionably *good* in climbing Mount Everest. The accomplishment of such a feat will elevate the human spirit. It will give men—and especially us geographers—a feeling that we really are getting the upper hand on the Earth, that we are acquiring a true mastery of our surroundings. As long as we impotently creep about at the foot of these mighty mountains and gaze on their summits without attempting to ascend them, we entertain towards them a too excessive feeling of awe. We are almost afraid of them. We have a secret fear that they, the material, are dominating us, the spiritual. But as soon as we have stood on their summit we feel that *we* dominate *them*—that we, the spiritual, have ascendancy over them, the material. And if man stands on Earth's highest summit he will have an increased pride and confidence in himself in his struggle for ascendancy over matter. This is the incalculable good which the ascent of Mount Everest will confer.

We who have lived among the peoples of the Himalaya are better able than most to appreciate how great this good is. We have seen how tame and meagre is their spirit in comparison with the spirit of, for example, the Swiss, or French, or Italian inhabitants of the Alps; and in comparison with what men's spirit ought to be. They have many admirable qualities, but they are fearful and unenterprising. Contact with them brings home to us what a spirit of daring and high adventure means to a people. And we are impressed with the necessity of taking every step possible to create, sustain, and strengthen this spirit in a people and in the human race generally. The ascent of Mount Everest, we believe, will be a big step in that direction.

The actual climbing of this mountain this Society will leave in the hands of the Alpine Club, who have special experience in mountain climbing. But the reconnaissance and mapping of the mountain and its neighbourhood will fitly remain with us. And here we reach the point where the principles I have been offering for your consideration might be applied. Were it not that the size of the first party will have to be limited on account of transport and supply difficulties, I should greatly like to have a poet or a painter, or anyhow a climber like Mr. Freshfield with a poetic soul, a member of it. For I say quite deliberately and mean quite literally that the geography of Mount Everest and its vicinity will not be complete until it has been painted by some great painter and described by some great poet. Making the most accurate map of it will not be completing our knowledge of it. The map-maker only prepares the way—in some cases for the soldier or the politician or the engineer—in this case for the geologist, the naturalist, and above all for the painter and poet. Until we have a picture and a poem—in prose or verse—of Mount Everest we shall not really know it; our Geography will be incomplete, and, indeed, will lack its chief essential.

The Duke of the Abruzzi, in his expedition to the second highest mountain in the world, took with him the finest mountain photographer there is—Signor

Vittorio Sella—and he brought back superb photographs, for he is a true artist with a natural feeling for high mountains. But I have seen the very mountains that he photographed, and when I look at these photographs—the best that man can produce—I almost weep to think how little of the real character of great mountains they communicate to us. The sight of the photographs wrings me with disappointment that it was a photographer and not a painter who went there. Here in Europe are artists by the score painting year after year the same old European scenes. And there in the Himalaya is the grandest scenery in the world, and not a painter from Europe ever goes there—except just one, the great Russian Verestchagin, whose pictures, alas! are now buried somewhere in Russia. The Indian Services might do something, and they have indeed produced one great painter of Himalayan scenery, Colonel Tanner. But the Services are limited, and it is to Europe that we must mainly look.

On the first expedition to Mount Everest it may be only possible to send a photographer. But this will be a pioneering expedition to open the way, at least, for the painter. And then we may have Mount Everest pictured in all her varied and ever-varying moods, as I have, from a distance, seen her for three most treasured months. Now serene and majestic; now in a tumult of fury. Now rooted solid on earth; now hung high in the azure. Now hard and material; now ethereal as spirit. Now stern and austere—cold, and white, and grey; now warm and radiant and of every most delicate hue. Now in one aspect, now in its precisely opposite, but always sublime and compelling; always pure and unspotted; and always pointing us starward.

These are the pictures—either by painter or by poet—that we want. And they can only be painted by one who has himself gone in among the mountains, confronted them squarely, braced himself against them, faced and overcome them—realised their greatness, realised also that great as they are he is greater still.

And this that we want of the greatest natural feature of the Earth is only typical of what this Society should require in regard to all Earth's other features in order to make our Geography complete. As men have pictured the loveliness of England, the fairness of France, the brilliance of Greece, so we want them to picture the spaciousness of Arabia, the luxuriance of Brazil, and the sublimity of the Himalaya. For not till that has been done will our Geography be complete. But when that has been accomplished and the quest for Beauty is being pushed to the remotest lands and Earth's farthest corners, even the British schoolboy will love his Geography, and our science will have won its final triumph. At nothing less, then, than the heart of the boy should our Society deign to aim.

AN ADDRESS TO THE UNION SOCIETY OF THE UNIVERSITY COLLEGE, LONDON, DELIVERED ON MARCH 17, 1921.

You have been good enough to leave to me the choice of subject on which to address you this evening, and I have chosen the subject "Natural Beauty and Geography" because I have the honour to hold at present the position of President of the Royal Geographical Society, and am therefore supposed to know something about Geography, and because a love of Natural Beauty is one of the great passions of my life.

I believe the two are inseparably connected with one another, and, briefly, the view I want to put before you is this—.that a description of the Natural Beauty of the Earth should be included in Geography. By Geography we mean a *description* of the Earth. And we cannot adequately describe the Earth until we have observed it in all its aspects and really know and understand it. And we cannot really understand the Earth until we have entered into her spirit and feel ourselves in harmony with it. But *when* our spirit is in harmony with the spirit of the Earth we, in that instant, see the Beauty of the Earth. When we are seeing Beauty in the Earth we are understanding the Earth. In describing the Beauty of the Earth we shall be describing something that we really know about it—something of the real nature of the Earth.

For this reason I maintain that Geography should be taken to include a description of the Natural Beauty of the Earth's features. The description of the Earth is not full and complete, and is lacking in its most important particular, when it excludes a description of Natural Beauty, and only includes scientific details about the size and shape of the earth; its configuration; the composition of the crust; the depth, area, and volume of the ocean; the temperature, degree of moisture and pressure of the atmosphere; the height of the mountains; the length, breadth, volume, course, and catchment area of its rivers; the mineral and vegetable products of various regions; the political areas into which it is divided; the relation of the political and commercial activities of the population to the physical character of the features and to the climate. I, of course, acknowledge the importance of all this geographical knowledge. To the historian and the statesman it is essential that he should know the part which a certain mountain range or river or desert has played in human history. A soldier must know with extreme accuracy the configuration of the country over which his army is operating. An engineer must know the exact level and contour of a region over which he has to lay a railway or construct a canal. A merchant must know whether a country produces cotton, tea, and sugar; or wheat, wool, and meat. For all these and others, each for his own particular purpose, we want the kind of information I have described above—that is, what usually goes under the name of Geography. But the point I wish now to urge is that we shall not have plucked the very flower of geographical knowledge until in addition to all this we have a knowledge of the *Beauty* of the Earth.

Perhaps you will understand me better if I illustrate my point. When a dressmaker has to make a dress for a lady she has to measure her with the minutest accuracy. She must gain a knowledge, by careful measurement, of the exact shape and size of the lady's body, its true contour, and the length and breadth of the limbs—just as an engineer must have accurate knowledge of the Earth's surface. And to the dressmaker *as* a dressmaker knowledge of the lady›s beauty has no value whatever. The lady may have the beauty of form of a Venus, but if the dressmaker has only knowledge of that beauty and has not exact measurements she will never be able to make the dress. But for humanity at large—and, as far as that goes, for the dressmaker herself when she is free of her dressmaking—knowledge of the lady's beauty is the knowledge that really matters. Whether she is twenty-six inches round the waist or only twenty-five matters comparatively little.

Now the Earth I regard as a lady—as dear Mother-Earth. A real living being—live enough, at any rate, to give birth to mankind, to microscopic animalculae first and through them to man. And no one can look at the features of Mother-Earth without recognising her Beauty. It is there staring us in the face. So I cannot conceive why we geographers should confine ourselves to the dressmaker attitude of mind and describe every other characteristic of the Earth except her Beauty. I should have thought that it was the very first thing with which we should have concerned ourselves—that the first duty of those who profess and call themselves geographers should have been to describe the beauty of their Mother-Earth.

Say a visitor from Mars arrived upon the Earth, he would no doubt report on his return that the mountains here were so many thousands of feet high and the seas so many thousands of feet deep, and the area of the land and sea so many thousand square miles; that the productivity of the land in one quarter had had the effect of attracting a large part of the population to that quarter, and the aridity or cold of another portion had had the effect of preventing human settlement there; and that mountains, seas, or deserts confining certain groups of human beings tightly within given areas had had the effect of compacting them into highly organised political bodies. All this and much more geographical knowledge the Martian would bring back to Mars. But his fellow-Martians would tell him that this was all very interesting, but that what they really wanted to know was what the Earth was *like*. They would ask him if he had not some lantern slides of the Earth, some photographs, something which would convey to them an impression of the real character of the Earth. And then at last he would be driven to describe her Beauty.

In the best words he could find he would express the impression which the Earth had made upon him. If he were a painter and if the Martians possess paint, he would paint pictures to express the feelings which a contemplation of the Earth had aroused in him. That is, he would show them the Beauty of the Earth in her various aspects. Perhaps he might not be able to see as much Beauty in her as we her children see. We may be too partial and see beauties that a stranger may not perceive. On the other hand, he might see beauties that we through being so accustomed to them have never recognised—as men living always within sight of some superb mountain scarcely appreciate its grandeur. Anyhow, he would describe to the Martians whatever he had seen of the Beauty of the Earth, and then at last they would feel that they were really able to know and understand her.

To descend from these celestial spheres and to examine what actually happens among ourselves when we venture into an unknown portion of this globe and seek to know what is there, a chief ingredient in the lure which draws men on to fill up the blank spaces in the map is undoubtedly a love of Natural Beauty; and its Natural Beauty is certainly what above everything else regarding that region remains in their memories after it has been explored. It is not *only* love of Natural Beauty that draws men on. Love of adventure has much to do with it also. Men feel a fearful joy in pitting themselves against stern natural obstacles and being compelled to exert all their physical energy and endurance, and all their wit and nerve and courage, in order to overcome them. The stiffer the obstacle, the more insistent do they feel the call to measure themselves against it. They thrill to the expectation of having their full capacities and faculties drawn out. By some curious natural instinct they seem driven to put themselves into positions where they are forced to exert themselves to the full stretch of their capabilities. This same instinct tells them that they will be never so happy as when they are making the very utmost of themselves and exercising their whole being at its highest pitch. Anticipation of their joy in adventure is therefore no small part of the lure which draws men into the unknown. And with it also is ambition to make a name and achieve fame. Some, too, are drawn on by the hope of wealth through finding gold, diamonds, and so on. But from what I have seen of gold and diamond prospectors on the spot in the act of prospecting, I should say it was quite as much love of adventure as covetousness of wealth that drew them into unknown parts. For experience shows them only too often that it is not the prospector but the company promoter and financier who make the money even when the prospector finds the gold or diamonds. Yet prospectors go forward as cheerfully as ever. They are fascinated by the life of adventure.

All this is true. Men delight in sheer adventure and in testing and sharpening themselves against formidable natural obstacles. Yet we shall find that love of Natural Beauty has an even greater share than love of adventure in enticing them to the unknown. Men picture to themselves beauties of the most wonderful kind which they expect to see—enchanting islands, mysterious forests, majestic rivers, heavenly mountains, delightful lakes. Instinct tells them that they will have the joy which comes from exerting their capacities to the full. But somewhere in the back of their being is, also this expectation of seeing wonders of Natural Beauty, and of seeing *more* of this Beauty from the very fact that they will be seeing it as a prize truly *won* and when their faculties are all tuned up to a fine pitch of appreciation.

And when they return from the unknown, when the adventure is over, when they are again relaxed, it will be the Natural Beauty which they have seen that will remain in their memories long after they have forgotten their exertion, long after they have expended any wealth they may have found, long after they have recorded the exact measurements of the various features of the region.

Curiosity to see the Natural Beauty of an unknown region is a principal ingredient in the lure that draws men to it. And Natural Beauty is what, above everything else in regard to the unknown region, stands out in men's memories on their return.

This at any rate is my own experience, and we are perhaps on safer ground when we speak of what we have ourselves experienced than when we speak of what we imagine must be the experiences of others. Though in this case I have good reason to believe that my own experiences are very similar to the experiences of others, and may therefore be taken as typical.

Almost my earliest recollections are of a Somersetshire village set in a lovely valley, fringed with woods and surrounded by hills. Up the hills on the side of the valley on which I lived I used constantly to go. But over the hills on the far side of the river I was never taken. So I used to picture to myself wonderful woods and rivers, and castles and great cities, and I longed to go there. The lure of Natural Beauty was beginning to make itself felt. As I grew to boyhood I was fortunate enough to be taken to North Wales, Devonshire and Cornwall, and later on to Switzerland and the South of France, and everywhere I saw much Natural Beauty. But, still, that only made me want to see more.

In all these cases, however, I only went where I was taken. I did not go where I chose or with an object of my own. It was not till I was in India and had the first leave from my regiment that I could go where I liked. Now, where I liked was to the Himalaya. And if I look back now and enquire of myself what made me choose the Himalaya, I can say most clearly that it was because I had in my mind a vision of long snowy ranges, and dazzling peaks, and frowning precipices, and rushing torrents, and endless forests. I thought how glorious it would be to be able to wander about at will and see all the magnificent scenery, to feast on the Natural Beauty, and when I came back to be able to tell others of the wonders I had seen.

So I made my first short trip in the Himalaya. But this only served to arouse my curiosity still more. I had seen some great mountains. But they were none of them more than 20,000 feet in height. I wanted to see still higher mountains. I heard, too, that up the valley of the Sutlej were some fearful gorges through which the river forced its way. I wanted to see them too, and see a great river in the very act of forcing its way through the mighty Himalaya. Above all, I wanted to see what lay on the other side of the Himalaya. I wanted to get into Tibet.

That for the time being proved impossible, and my thoughts wandered off to the far eastern part of Asia. I had read a book called "On the Amur," by Atkinson. Not altogether a very veracious book, but a fascinating book for all that. In it were alluring pictures of the broad, placid river. Rich forests came down to the water's edge. And on its surface were depicted delightful rafts and canoes. To glide down such a river, to camp on its banks and plunge into the forests which clothed them, seemed a joy second only to the joy of scrambling about the Himalaya. So with Mr. H. E. M. James—now Sir Evan James—I went to Manchuria, not, indeed, to reach the Amur itself, but to discover the source of its great tributary the Sungari, and to follow it down through the forests and over the plains for several hundred miles.

Now, what I want to impress upon you is that in all these cases it was the Natural Beauty which was the attraction—it was the picture I made to myself of what these countries would be like that drew me on. And I am sure it is with others as it was with me. Natural Beauty is at bottom what incites the traveller.

And, whether I had to go where I was taken or could go where I chose, it was the Natural Beauty that stuck in my memory. And when I returned it was of the Natural Beauty that I wished to tell my friends. And this, again, is the experience of others also. To this day, though I have never since seen them, I remember the beauties of Cader Idris and Dolgelly, Snowdon and Carnarvon, in North Wales, and of the rugged cliffs and long Atlantic waves on the Cornish coast. The Dart, here rippling over boulders and between rocky banks, here in deep, clear salmon pools, here merging into a long inlet of the sea and everywhere framed in wooded hill-sides, I have often again seen. But even if I had not, its beauty would never have departed from my memory. And it is the same with the first view of the Alps from the Jura, the view of Lake Geneva, of the Jungfrau, of the Pyrenees from Pau, and of the valley of the Loire. I have never seen those parts of Switzerland and of France since then, but their beauty remains with me to this day. And it is of their beauty that I have ever afterwards been naturally inclined to speak. When I talk about the Loire I do not tell my friends that it rises in a certain place, is so many miles long, at certain parts has a certain width, depth, and volume, and eventually flows into a certain sea. What I naturally speak about is its beauty, the rich valley through which it flows, the graceful bridges by which it is spanned, the picturesque old towns and romantic castles on the banks. And this is the common habit of mankind. Our friends may bore us—and we may bore our friends—with interminable accounts of the discomfort and inconveniences and the petty little incidents of travel. But when they and we have got through that and settle down to describe the country itself, it is of its beauty that we speak.

Natural Beauty is what attracts us to a country. Its Natural Beauty is the fact about it which remains most persistently in our memory. And it is about its Natural Beauty that we are most inclined to speak. Lastly, when we are in distant countries it is of the Natural Beauty that we chiefly think. When our thoughts go back to the home country it is not on its exact measurements and configuration that they dwell, but on its beauty.

From all of which considerations I conclude that any description of the Earth which excludes a description of its Natural Beauty is incomplete. Geography must include a description of Natural Beauty. And personally I would go so far as to say that the description of Natural Beauty is the most important part of Geography.

Here I must answer an objection which may be raised—namely, that Natural Beauty is the concern of Aesthetics, not of Geography. An objector may freely acknowledge the value and importance of recognising and describing the Natural Beauty of a country, but may contend that this is beyond the province of Geography. It should be left to poets and painters, he might say, and geographers should confine themselves to the more prosaic business of exact measurement, of accurate delineation, of reasoning regarding the relation of the facts to one another, and of explaining the facts.

To such an objector I would reply that Geography is an art as well as a science. And in parenthesis I may say that I doubt whether any science can be complete which has not art behind it. We shall never be able fully to know and understand the Earth or to describe what we see if we use our intellectual and reasoning powers alone. If we are to attain to a complete knowledge of the Earth, and if we are to describe what we learn about it in an adequate manner so that others may participate in our knowledge, then we must use our hearts as well as our heads. We must be artists as well as meticulous classifiers, cataloguers, and reasoners. The Earth is a living being, a throbbing, palpitating, living being—"live" enough to have given birth to the remote ancestors of mankind, and live enough, so some biologists consider, to be continually to this day generating the lowliest forms of organisms. To know and understand a living being, particularly when that living being happens to be his own Mother, man must use his heart as well as his head.

With his head alone the geographer may do a vast amount of most useful and necessary work which will help us to understand the Earth. He may collect and classify facts about her and record measurements, and reason about these facts and measurements, but if he is to get the deepest vision of the Earth and learn the profoundest truth about her he must exercise his finest spiritual senses as well. And when he brings those faculties of the soul into play, it will be the Beauty on the face of Mother-Earth that he will see and that will disclose to him her real nature.

And therefore I hold that if it be the function of Geography to know the Earth and to describe the Earth, then the objection that the description of its Natural Beauty is outside the scope of Geography is not a valid objection. The picture and the poem are as legitimate a part of Geography as the map.

Some years ago in lecturing to the Royal Geographical Society I said that the Society ought to have given Wordsworth the Gold Medal. I meant that the poet by his vision had taught us more about the Lake District than any ordinary geographer had been able to see. With his finer sensibility he had been able to see deeper. He had been able to reveal to us truths about the district which no mere ordnance surveyor was able to disclose. He was a true discoverer—a geographical discoverer—a geographer of the highest type. He had helped us really to know and understand the district.

Be it noted, too, that he did not, as some would think, put into the lakes and hills and valleys something from within himself which was not really in those natural features. The particular beauty that he saw there was there waiting to be revealed. The natural features aroused emotions in his sensitive soul, and his soul being aroused saw the beauty in them. If the district had been of billiard-table flatness, with no lakes, no hills, no valleys, then even he, with all his poetic feeling and imagination, could not have put into the district what it did not possess. The beauty that he saw was really there, only it required a poetic soul to discover and reveal it. The spirit of the poet put itself in touch with the spirit of the district and elicited from the district what was already in it. The spirit of Wordsworth and the spirit of the district acted and reacted upon one another and came into harmony with one another. And as he had the capacity for communicating to others what he himself had seen, we are now able to see in the Lakeland beauties which our forefathers had scarcely known.

This is why I suggest to you that Natural Beauty should be considered as a legitimate part of Geography. And if you will look about you, you will note that Natural Beauty is having an increasing effect upon the movements of men. There is a very definite relationship between the Beauty of the Earth and her human inhabitants. The Poet Laureate builds his house on the top of Boar's Hill not because the soil is specially productive up there so that he may be able to grow food, for the soil is rather poor; not because water is easily available, for it is very difficult to get, as he found when his house took fire; not because of the climate, for the climate is just as good a hundred feet lower down; not because it is easily accessible to Oxford, for a big climb up the hill is entailed every time he returns from that city—not for any of these reasons did he build his house there, but because of the view which he obtains from that spot. It was Natural Beauty which drew, the Poet Laureate to Boar's Hill, as it was Natural Beauty which drew Tennyson to Blackdown to build Aldworth with a view all over the Surrey hills and the Sussex Downs.

It is this same spell of Natural Beauty, too, which is drawing people all over England to build their houses on the most beautiful spots. Our great country-seats—the pride of England—are usually placed where the natural scenery is finest. Humbler dwellings whenever the owner has the opportunity of making a choice are for a similar reason built wherever a beautiful view, however limited, may be obtained. Whole towns even are built on spots where the surroundings are most beautiful, or, at any rate, if for some other reason they were located where they are they tend to spread in the direction of most beauty. Dartmouth was originally built where it is because that site made an excellent port. But the new town has spread all over the cliffs at the entrance of the harbour wherever a beautiful view may be found. It is the same with Torquay. People originally went there on account of the warm, soft air. But though they can get much the same air in any part of the Torquay area, where they like to build their houses is where they can get the finest views.

On the Continent a similar tendency may be observed. Nice, Cannes, Monte Carlo, Biarritz, Montreux, Vevey, were no doubt originally located where they are for other reasons than only the facilities they afford for observing Natural Beauty, but that they have grown to what they are is undoubtedly due to Natural Beauty, and Natural Beauty has given the direction in which they have expanded. It is not by chance that villas and terraces and hotels have been built just on those particular points from which the most beautiful views may be seen.

And how great is the influence of Natural Beauty upon the movements of men may be gathered from the amount of money railway companies and hotels spend in advertising the charms of the particular localities which they serve. Railway-carriages are full of photographs and tourist agencies of pictures of different points in the neighbourhood of the railway or hotel. And we may be certain that business companies would not go to the expense of setting up these photographs and pictures if they did not think that people were influenced by them and would be tempted to travel to the scenes they depict.

The development of char-a-banc tours is another indication of the attraction—and the increasing attraction—of Natural Beauty. Since the War, especially, there has been a remarkable tendency of people of every rank in life to rush off whenever they can get a holiday to the most beautiful parts of these islands—to the moors of Yorkshire and Devonshire, to the Wye, the Dart, and the Severn, to the mountains of Wales, Westmoreland, and Scotland—to wherever Natural Beauty may be found. It is a noteworthy and most refreshing feature in our national life.

Every summer, too, both here and on the Continent, people make their way to the most beautiful parts of Europe—to Switzerland or the Pyrenees, the Vosges or the Rhine. And in the Dominions and America whenever they get their holidays they likewise trek away to mountain, lake, or river, wherever Nature may be enjoyed at her best. Men may, to carry on the ordinary business of life, be compelled to live in cities and places which are chosen for other reasons than their facilities for observing Natural Beauty. But whenever they can get away from their ordinary duties the tendency of men—and a tendency increasing in strength—is to fly away to the moors and sea-coast and river-sides and wherever else they can see the beauties of the Earth.

Then, again, men are increasingly sensitive about preserving Natural Beauty wherever it is best. It is quite true that men by the building of industrial towns and the erection of hideous factories, mining plant, gasometers, and so on terribly destroy Natural Beauty. But they are at least becoming conscious of their sins in this respect and of what they have lost thereby. They are therefore the more anxious to preserve what remains. And whenever there is an attempt to build on Box Hill, or erect an electric power-station on Dartmoor, a howl of execration is raised. And this howl means that men do value Natural Beauty and mean to preserve it.

Young countries also realise its value. In California the Yosemite Valley is preserved for ever for human enjoyment. And in Canada, Australia, and South Africa national parks are protected against the encroachments of industrial enterprises.

Men not only preserve spots of Natural Beauty; they also seek to improve them. The nobleman of ancient lineage and the new millionaire alike strive to add to the beauty of their estates. The hours they love best are the hours they can devote to opening up vistas, planting beautiful trees or flowering shrubs from distant lands, building up rockeries, forming artificial lakes, laying out lawns, and stocking their gardens with the choicest flowers.

The effect of Natural Beauty upon man and of man upon Natural Beauty is immense. Geographers take note of the effect which the Alps by reason of their height and ruggedness, or the Rhine by reason of its length, breadth, and depth, have upon the activities of men—upon their history, politics, and economic life. My contention is that equally should geographers note the effect which these same natural features of the Earth by reason of their *beauty* have upon men›s activities and movements.

And when Natural Beauty is fully recognised as within the province of Geography, we shall be taught to pay to it the attention it deserves—taught to look for it, taught how to observe it, taught how to describe it, taught where are the regions of special beauty and wherein their beauty lies, and lastly taught where in an ordinary district Beauty may be found, for even in the flattest, dreariest region *some* beauty at some time of day or at some season may be discovered. We shall, in short, be taught to cultivate the sense for Natural Beauty, and how to put in fitting words a description of the beauty we see. Our geography textbooks, besides all the mathematical, physical, political, and commercial geography they contain, will tell us something of the Natural Beauty of the countries they set themselves to describe. And geographers when they set themselves to describe a new region will not think it necessary to confine themselves within the old limits, but will do what the ordinary man instinctively does—describe its beauties.

Our methods of describing countries will thus radically change. A few years ago Colonel Tanner of the Survey of India read to the Royal Geographical

Society a paper entitled "Our Present Knowledge of the Himalaya." In that paper he gave an account of the height of the peaks, the trend of the mountain ranges, the course of the rivers, and a deal of other very valuable geographical information. But in only one single line did he make any remark about the natural beauty of that wonderful region. Yet this omission was not due to any lack of appreciation by Colonel Tanner of Himalayan beauty, for he himself had painted the finest pictures of the Himalaya which have yet been produced. He made no mention of it because he thought that to describe the natural beauty of the Himalaya was to stray beyond the bounds of Geography.

Such a grievous misconception of the true scope of Geography will, I trust, be removed in future. And when it no longer exists Geography will require for its pursuit the exercise of the finest faculties of the soul as well as the strictest qualities of the intellect. It will call forth capacity for the closest and most accurate observation and the highest powers of description. To us adventure-loving and Nature-loving Englishmen it should of all subjects be the most popular.